Dialogues on Miracle

Dialogues on Miracle

ROBERT A. LARMER

FOREWORD BY GARY R. HABERMAS

WIPF & STOCK · Eugene, Oregon

DIALOGUES ON MIRACLE

Wipf & Stock
An Imprint of Wipf and Stock Publishers
199 W. 8th Ave., Suite 3
Eugene, OR 97401

www.wipfandstock.com

ISBN 13: 978-1-62564-816-7

Manufactured in the U.S.A.

For my children,
Anna, Robb, Jer, and Nome

CONTENTS

FOREWORD

by Gary R. Habermas

ROBERT A. LARMER IS professor and chair of the Philosophy Department at the University of New Brunswick, in Canada. Bob is a longtime specialist and contributor to philosophical discussions regarding the subject of miracles. Having written a number of focused works on the subject,[1] he has in this work, very successfully in my opinion, treated us to a most delightful fictional dialogue, following in a long line of philosophical works of this nature. It is amazing that so many influential philosophical ideas have been conveyed over the centuries via dialogue, and the format lends itself nicely to use with undergraduate students as the protagonists.

THE CONTEMPORARY SCENE

Are miracles even possible? How might they be defined? Is there any chance that they have actually occurred in the time-space world of past generations? Perhaps most interesting of all, might miracles be taking place in the present? Some may be surprised to learn that questions such as these are not solely the simple concerns of sectarian religious folks but are also of great interest to contemporary scholars. During the last few decades there have

---

1. One of his most recent publications on the topic is *The Legitimacy of Miracle.*

been literally thousands of sophisticated publications on these and other related issues, written by believers and unbelievers alike.

More specifically, a huge change has occurred in recent studies of the historical Jesus. Today, the majority critical position is that Jesus indeed did either perform many of the miraculous events recorded about him in the Gospels, or at least did things that were very much like those. Quite surprisingly, even well-known skeptical scholar Marcus Borg asserts that, "despite the difficulty which miracles pose for the modern mind, on historical grounds it is virtually indisputable that Jesus was a healer and exorcist."[2]

What about present-day miracles—are there any such events? Several studies have been published, some with scientific accounts accompanied by strong pre- and post-data gathered from CT scans, MRIs, and X-rays, documenting the measurable changes in individuals in the immediate presence of prayer or other religious pointers, often in front of physicians. Craig Keener in his recent two-volume work, *Miracles: The Credibility of the New Testament Accounts*, provides many of these evidenced cases.[3] More than one physician has also provided other incredible accounts, including the evidence.[4]

Perhaps as a result, several recent opinion polls indicate another direction to this topic. Apparently, a major shift may be under way in many segments of the population, among a wide swath of our society, both professional and otherwise, regarding belief in the reality of miraculous events. For example, in the medical community, long thought by some to be among the more skeptical professions regarding the existence of supernatural realities, a 2004 survey reported that a majority of medical doctors both thought that miracles happened in the past (74%), and that they could also occur in the present (73%). Moreover, most of these physicians (59%) pray for their patients, and a majority (55%) even reported

2. Borg, *Jesus, a New Vision*, 61.

3. For just a few of the details, see Keener, *Miracles*, 1:428–35, 440, 463, 491, 503; 2:206, 680.

4. Casdorph, *Real Miracles: Indisputable Medical Evidence That God Heals.* Also Gardner, *Healing Miracles: A Doctor Investigates.*

that they had witnessed personally what they considered to be miracles that had occurred among their own patients![5]

However, in my PhD course entitled "Miracles," we begin by considering some dozen-and-a-half skeptical a priori objections of various sorts to the belief in supernatural events, as represented in major academic journals. This much attention from critical scholars is compelling evidence that far more than believers alone are interested in the subject of miracle.

Even if a majority of people today, including physicians, believe in miracles, this is not to demonstrate that they are justified in such belief. What it does signal is that the appearance of new empirical evidence is potentially a major factor in making the possibility of justified belief in miracles more of an open question right now than it has been in a very long time. Bob, in this volume, takes on the task of making accessible to the non-specialist the central philosophical issues that arise in considering the rationality of belief in miracles. One of his major contributions to the debate has been to argue that many philosophers have been far too ready to dismiss on a priori grounds the occurrence of miracles, rather than to deal with empirical data.

THE SETTING OF THIS VOLUME

This particular fictional discussion takes place in the setting of seven consecutive meetings of an undergraduate philosophy club, called the Socrates Society. It convenes on a university campus and the students have agreed for a term to carry on an open philosophical dialogue regarding the topic of "whether belief in miracles could ever be rationally justified" (chap 1, p. 1). Although most philosophy professors might wish their students more resembled Bob's fictional characters, the discussions we find in the various dialogues are not stilted or otherwise difficult to grasp.

---

5. These data are reported by Keener, *Miracles*, 2:721–22. Several other surveys with both positive and very intriguing results are reported by Keener in 1:204–5.

The student participants throughout the volume are Mary (a fourth-year philosophy honors student), John (another fourth-year philosophy honors student), Susan (the incoming Socrates Society president and a third-year philosophy honors student), Brendan (a third-year history honors student), and Holly (a second-year psychology major), who frequently requests that the philosophy students be more helpful in defining their in-house verbiage. The group is joined by Professor Roberts, their faculty advisor, who suggested the theme for the term and often supplies definitions and background information, especially for the non-philosophy majors.

Throughout, the student discussion is crisp, succinct, and generally stays on task. When it begins to wander slightly, just a few times, President Susan or Professor Roberts gently direct the others back to the chief topic for that particular meeting. A reading from a portion of David Hume's famous essay "Of Miracles" quite often provides the backdrop and focal point of that week's discussion. Objections to one another are posed, honed, argued, and not always solved to everyone's satisfaction, just as in real-life philosophical dialogue! The discussion is fair and regularly provides both positive as well as negative critiques. In the end, students and readers alike are left to draw their final conclusions.

Time and again, it is easy for the reader to imagine being present at the discussion as a member of the group, like one might be drawn into a good philosophically-inclined novel. The more the reader is acquainted with the subject matter in current miracles discussions, the more often the opportunity will present itself to smile and think that the students are indeed following the appropriate topics through to their conclusions.

KEY IDEAS FOR FURTHER EXPLORATION

Throughout the dialogue, significant notions from current philosophical discussions on the topic of miracles emerge and are treated from more than one perspective. The overall effect is that, by enjoying the discussion, one becomes immersed in the relevant issues.

For example, it is quite frequently surmised by both believers and unbelievers alike that miracles, by definition, should be defined as events that violate the laws of nature in a strong sense, or at least temporarily supersede these laws in some weaker sense. Thus, the skeptical philosopher David Hume argued that such events should be defined as violations of nature's laws.

But in chapters 1 and 2, Mary in particular argues that divine intervention could occur in such a way so as to produce an event that nature would not otherwise produce on its own, but which would not necessarily violate nature's laws in the process. Common examples from everyday life are marshaled in making her case. Much rides on the conclusion here, for if Mary is correct in her contentions, then common Humean-type arguments based on the balance of probabilities which seek to juxtapose the evidence for the laws of nature over against the testimonial evidence in favor of miracles perhaps cannot even get started. This could be the case, she points out, since these skeptical arguments are built on the assumption that there is a conflict between nature's laws and the human testimony, which need not necessarily be so at all.

Another important issue in this dialogue (in chaps. 5 and 6) is the question of whether an unusual event that has occurred must be distinguished from what is the best explanation of such an event. Given that there is good evidence for deciding that certain events that have traditionally been understood as miracles have actually occurred, the progress of science may actually strengthen the claim that these should be considered miraculous.

For example, there is no question that we know far more about human physiology and chemistry than we did two thousand years ago, but none of this increased knowledge has made it any easier to produce a natural explanation of an event such as Jesus turning water into wine simply by giving the command, or especially his rising from the dead.

Along the way, other vital topics are introduced and discussed by the students. Chapter 3 is devoted to the strength of Hume's a priori argument against miracles as presented in section 1 of his essay on miracles, while chapter 4 is concerned with Hume's a posteriori arguments as presented in section 2 of the same essay. Chapter 5 introduces the crucial topic of methodological naturalism and whether scientific study requires that natural causes be assumed for all events. John argues that, without that, science simply cannot operate properly. Holly quips that such a requirement "sounds like methodological atheism to me."

Chapter 6 concerns another central topic: whether Hume was correct in postulating that a miracle can never serve as an argument for the existence of God or for the truth of a particular theological system. As is often the case, John is the chief defender of Hume, while Mary presents several contrary arguments. Some crucial distinctions are made in this discussion, such as a miracle being a type of teleological argument. Lastly, chapter 7 poses the thorny issue of what bearing the possibility of miracles might have on subjects often associated with the problem of evil and whether God may have created an imperfect world that necessitates his tampering.

CONCLUSION

Several times while reading this volume, it occurred to me that a book of this nature was an excellent means of getting across key ideas in this philosophical discussion and doing so in a lively way that moves quickly, apart from the normally extended and detailed theoretical diatribes that often lose students in the process. The final result, in my opinion, is elegant, delightful, and, in the end, very instructional. Suggestions are made, answered, and repackaged, just as these sorts of dialogues happen in everyday life.

Any final judgments are left open-ended, and no force-feeding occurs. The reader can creatively take the side of any of the students, or take a different approach altogether, pose their own responses, and then shift sides to argue the opposite view. Is it true that David Hume seems to get the "short end of the stick" in this discussion, just as he does in so many other philosophical discussions of late? Is that justified? Why or why not does this seem to be the case? Each reader may interact with the discussion, evaluate the arguments, and then decide who makes the better case. All that is asked of the reader is that he or she be open to rational discussion of an important and interesting topic.

PREFACE

THE LITERARY DEVICE OF dialogue is a time-honored means of exploring philosophical questions. We find it employed by philosophers of the stature of Plato, Berkeley, and Hume, to name only a few of those who have used it to great effect. I propose to use it in this book as a way of exploring, in a manner that will be readily accessible to those with little or no formal training in philosophy, important questions concerning the rationality of belief in miracles.

A criticism that can be fairly raised is that, in many instances, "philosophical dialogues" are scarcely deserving of the term "dialogue." One hears in the central character the voice and views of the author, but the other characters in the dialogue often seem at best compliant or at worst inept. Done poorly, the philosophical dialogue highlights the very human tendency to overestimate the force of one's arguments and to underestimate or ignore criticisms of one's position.

One-sidedness is not, however, a necessary feature of the philosophical dialogue. Done well, a philosophical dialogue genuinely engages with the views its author opposes, making the best case that can be made for their acceptance, even while trying to show that, in the final analysis, they are in error. I make no secret of the fact that my goal in this book is to provide a philosophical defense of the possibility of rationally justified belief in miracles, and that my desire is to present this defense in such a way that it is readily comprehensible to the non-specialist in philosophy or theology. Such a defense can legitimately dispense with much of the paraphernalia that professional scholars in a discipline use in writing for other professional scholars in their discipline—some texts seem to be more references than argument—but it must not "dumb down" the material by oversimplifying the issues, or presenting "straw man" versions of the arguments it seeks to refute.

In my view, the literary device of philosophical dialogue presents an effective method of presenting philosophical issues to interested lay persons. With its many conversational turns, it allows the core issues of the discussion to be explored without getting lost in the detail that characterizes the work of professional academics writing for other professional academics. This is not to say that there is not an important role for such scholarly writing—I have written several books on the topic of miracle in which I engage other professional philosophers—but it is scarcely a recommendation of one's philosophical views if they cannot be made understandable to those outside the discipline. Indeed it seems essential that one be able to do this, since everyone holds philosophical positions whether they realize it or not. The danger is holding a position and being unaware that one holds it or that it is open to question.

I have set these dialogues in the context of a series of meetings of an undergraduate philosophy club known as the Socratic Society. The society's faculty advisor is Professor Roberts, who has suggested to the society that their meetings for the term be based around the theme of whether belief in miracles could ever be rational. In addition to Professor Roberts, I make use of five other characters.

> *Mary*: a fourth-year honors student in philosophy
>
> *John*: a fourth-year honors student in philosophy
>
> *Susan*: a third-year honors student in philosophy
>
> *Brendan*: a third-year honors student in history
>
> *Holly*: a second-year student majoring in psychology and
biology

Mary and John are responsible for the bulk of the conversation that occurs in the dialogues; Mary being an articulate Christian theist, and John being an articulate atheist. Susan, Brendan, and Holly have somewhat lesser roles; they participate in the discussion as individuals who have not previously thought much about the relative merits of theism and atheism, but who are interested in the question of whether belief in miracles might ever be justified. Professor Roberts functions as someone who explains the occasional technical term that slips into the conversation, and who prevents the conversation from venturing down side paths that, although important and interesting, would lead the participants too far astray from their topic of discussion.

Having introduced the characters, I invite you, the reader, to listen in, as it were, on a series of conversations. My hope is that they prove both enjoyable and illuminating.

1

Defining a Miracle

John, Mary, Susan, Brendan, Holly, and Professor Roberts are gathered together in the Philosophy Lounge.

Susan: As the incoming president, I want to welcome all of you to the first meeting this term of the Socrates Society, our undergraduate philosophy club. This term, on the advice of our faculty advisor to the club, Professor Roberts, we decided to devote our discussions to a single topic—namely, discussion of whether belief in miracles could ever be rationally justified. I suggest that in this, our first meeting, we begin by trying to get clear what we mean by the term "miracle."

Holly: I am not a philosophy student, but I am interested in religion and spirituality. I may get shot down, but to get the discussion started, I am going to say that a miracle is an amazing event.

John: I want to ask Holly a question.

Holly: Go ahead, but please remember that I just said that I am not a philosophy student.

John: Do you want to say that anything amazing is a miracle? What if some people find something amazing and others don't?

Holly: That is really two questions, but I guess I would say that something is a miracle if someone finds it amazing, but not a miracle if they don't.

Brendan: So you would say that what a religious believer calls a miracle, the non-believer might call luck or happy coincidence.

Holly: Yes, that sounds right.

Mary: It doesn't sound right to me. How could the same event be both a miracle and just luck or coincidence? Are you saying that the same event could be both a miracle and not a miracle? Isn't that just a contradiction?

Holly: I don't see why. The same event could be a miracle for one person, but not for another. It all depends on your point of view. It's a miracle if you think it is, but not a miracle if you don't.

John: Unlike Mary, I don't believe in God or the supernatural, but I always thought that a miracle was supposed to be caused by some supernatural intervention into nature.

Holly: Ok, but what is your point?

John: Well an amazing event is either caused by a supernatural intervention, say God, or it is not. It can't both be a supernatural intervention and not a supernatural intervention.

Holly: Why not? Who is to say whether something is a supernatural intervention or not? People should be allowed to make up their own minds on religious matters.

John: I agree that people should be allowed to make up their own minds, but that is not the point at issue. What I am claiming is that just saying an unusual or amazing event is a miracle is not enough to make it one.

Holly: I don't see why not. Who are you to say whether an amazing event was a supernatural intervention or not? How are you going to tell?

Prof. Roberts: I don't want to interrupt, but I think it would be helpful if we distinguish the question of what makes a claim true from the question of how we know it to be true.

Brendan: Like Holly, I am not a philosophy major. Can you explain what you just said so I can understand.

Prof. Roberts: Perhaps an example will help. Suppose you look out the window and see a young woman walking by. It will either be true or false that she is pregnant, but it may be difficult, or perhaps impossible, just by looking at her to know whether she is pregnant or not.

Holly: I am afraid I need more explanation. What is the point of the example?

Prof. Roberts: What I am trying to get at is that the question of how I know something to be true is a different question from what makes it true. To stick with our pregnancy example, a woman might find out that she is pregnant by taking a pregnancy test, but it would be a mistake to assume that it was the test that caused her to be pregnant.

Brendan: I get it. The question of whether an event was caused by a supernatural intervention is different from the question of whether supernatural interventions are easy to recognize.

Holly: I want to be sure I understand. Professor Roberts, are you saying that if we define a miracle as a supernatural intervention then an event is either a miracle or not, but sometimes it may not be easy to tell whether it was a miracle? So if someone has, say a cold and gets prayed for and the cold gets better really fast the getting better really fast is either the result of supernatural intervention or not. But since colds often get better quickly on their own it is hard to be sure if it is true that there was supernatural intervention or simply a lucky coincidence.

Prof. Roberts: Yes, how we come to know a claim to be true is a very different question from what makes it true. To take a different example, someone might come to know that Obama defeated Romney in the United States general election of 2012, through reading about it in the newspaper or on the internet. What makes it true that Obama defeated Romney, however, is that Obama got more Electoral College votes than did Romney.

Holly: I take your point, but that still does not explain why it would be wrong to view a miracle as a fortunate coincidence rather than a supernatural intervention. Why drag in the idea of the supernatural.

Brendan: When I think of a coincidence, I think of it as occurring by chance rather than design. I do not think of miracles as chance events that just happen; in my understanding, they are the result of deliberate action. Defining a miracle as a coincidence doesn't seem to fit with the idea of a supernatural agent causing it.

Mary: I agree with Brendan. Also, is getting better quickly from a cold a good example? When I think of a miracle I think of something pretty dramatic—things like healing someone of blindness or walking on water. Wouldn't it be pretty easy to recognize those types of events as supernatural interventions and wouldn't it be difficult to view them as just coincidences?

Holly: Ok, you have persuaded me that the notion of coincidence does not capture the idea that a miracle is caused by a supernatural agent and that we must define miracles in terms of supernatural intervention, but could not recovering from a cold quickly be just as much a result of supernatural intervention as walking on water?

Mary: Sure, but it is a whole lot easier to recognize walking on water as a supernatural intervention. I want to say that a miracle is a supernatural intervention that can be easily recognized.

Holly: What about ones that are not easily recognized? Why don't you want to call them miracles? I thought theists believe that God intervenes in little ways as well as big ways.

Mary: I think there are all sorts of little interventions by God, but they don't seem on a par with things like walking on water.

Prof. Roberts: How about reserving the term "miracle" for dramatic interventions that are easily recognized as such and calling less dramatic interventions and less easily recognized interventions something else?

Brendan: Like what?

Mary: You could call the less dramatic interventions providential events.

Brendan: So the difference between a miracle and a providential event is that a miracle is easily recognized as an intervention by God and a providential event is not?

John: Not that I believe in any of this stuff, but are you saying that a providential event has to be a supernatural intervention? Assuming God exists couldn't he providentially work through natural causes?

Brendan: I agree. Why think that God only works through divine intervention?

Prof. Roberts: I don't like to keep interrupting, but saying that some providential events are the result of supernatural intervention does not mean that you have to say all providential events are the result of supernatural intervention. Bear in mind that theists believe that God sometimes achieve his purposes through natural means and other times through supernatural means. Remember, though, that the question you are addressing is whether you want to reserve the term "miracle" for supernatural interventions that can be easily recognized. What is meant by calling something a providential event is an interesting question, but it is not the question you decided to discuss in these meetings.

Mary: I opt for defining a miracle as a dramatic supernatural intervention that can be easily recognized. That allows us to be more precise in describing what is meant by calling an event a miracle.

Susan: I have a question. Assuming there are dramatic supernatural interventions, why think they are caused by God? Could a miracle be caused by an angel or by the devil?

Brendan: Good question. Doesn't the Bible talk about evil spirits and their effects on the world?

Holly: Do people really take seriously that idea anymore? Don't educated people laugh at the idea of anybody taking evil spirits seriously.

Mary: That might just be cultural prejudice. Lots of intelligent people now and throughout history have taken their existence seriously.

John: I agree with Holly that it is difficult to take the idea of demons seriously, but if we are going down that road then Susan is right. Defining a miracle as a dramatic supernatural intervention doesn't guarantee that God did it or even that the intervention is good.

Brendan: It doesn't sound right to talk of evil miracles. Aren't miracles by definition supposed to be good?

John: Well you need to change your definition then.

Mary: How about this? A miracle is a dramatic supernatural intervention by God.

Susan: That would rule out the devil, but wouldn't it also mean that an angel couldn't do a miracle.

John: Why are you assuming there are angels or the devil or God?

Brendan: I don't think she is assuming that such beings exist. All Susan is asking is whether if angels do exist and intervene on nature, should that intervention be called a miracle.

Susan: Getting back to my question. Wouldn't we call a supernatural intervention by an angel a miracle?

John: You can't if you are defining a miracle as a supernatural intervention done by God.

Mary: Could we say that a miracle is a dramatic supernatural intervention done by God or an agent acting on God's behalf? Wouldn't that work?

John: Since I do not believe in the supernatural, I think this is all beside the point. But if you want to talk about the devil and bad angels, what about their interventions? What are you going to call those kinds of interventions.

Mary: Why not call them false miracles? Genuine miracles will be supernatural interventions in accordance with God's purposes. False miracles will be interventions that are not in line with God's purposes.

Susan: Does that mean that only angels or God can do miracles? Aren't there places in the Bible where humans are claimed to have performed miracles and don't some Christians think that saints do miracles? And I don't think that this is just true of Christianity; I think other religions make similar claims.

Mary: I am not sure whether people do miracles through their own power, but I don't think that matters. What I want to say is that a miracle is a dramatic supernatural intervention in accordance with God's purposes. That doesn't rule out persons performing miracles.

Holly: This all seems so nit-picky. Why not say that something is a miracle if you think it is a miracle.

Brendan: But then anything could be a miracle.

Holly: No, I don't mean that. It has to be something pretty special.

Brendan: But once you start saying a miracle has to be something pretty special we seem to be back to talking about definitions.

Holly: Ok, I just don't think it should be so complicated. Who are you to say your definition is better than my definition?

John: What exactly is your definition Holly?

Holly: Well it has to be unusual.

Brendan: That's where we started, remember. That's not going to work all by itself. I don't think we can escape being what you're calling nit-picky.

Holly: Ok I get the point. But do philosophers always have to make things so complicated? It reminds me of that joke about the millipede who was asked how he managed to walk with so many legs and once he started to think about it he never was able to walk again.

Mary: I am going with the definition that a miracle is a dramatic supernatural intervention in nature in accordance with God's purposes.

Brendan: Do we really need to build in the idea of a supernatural intervention? Why couldn't we define a miracle simply as an event without a natural cause?

Susan: For the same reason we cannot think of a miracle as simply a coincidence. A miracle is not just an event that cannot be explained in terms of natural causes, it is an event that has a supernatural cause.

John: I agree that we have to define a miracle as a supernatural intervention but what about the idea that a miracle is a violation of the laws of nature? It seems obvious that if a miracle is a supernatural intervention in nature, that the only way it could occur is to violate some law of nature. So shouldn't part of the definition of a miracle be that it is a violation of the laws of nature?

Susan: So your claim is that the only way a supernatural intervention can take place is by violating, that is to say, breaking, a law of nature.

John: Exactly. And that means that any definition of miracle must include the idea that miracles violate the laws of nature.

Mary: But isn't the basic idea that of divine intervention in nature rather than violation of a law of nature?

John: I'm not sure what you're getting at?

Mary: Well, being a supernatural intervention is essential for something to be a miracle, but violating a law of nature will only be essential for something to be a miracle if it is true that this is the only way supernatural interventions can occur.

Holly: Talk about logic-chopping. Next you will be discussing how many angels can dance on the head of a pin.

Susan: Hold on Holly, Mary is making an important point. You can't just assume that the only way a miracle can occur is by violating a law of nature. That means you can't simply assume that miracle should be defined as violating a law of nature.

Holly: But why is that important?

Prof. Roberts: I agree that Mary's point is important. A lot of criticisms of belief in miracle—I think especially of David Hume—depend on the assumption that miracles should be defined as violating laws of nature. If it turns out that miracles could occur without violating any laws of nature this might undermine those criticisms.

John: But to use Holly's phrase, isn't Mary just nit-picking? It's pretty clear that the only way a supernatural intervention can take place is to violate the laws of nature. Does anyone suppose that the virgin birth of Jesus would not violate at least one law of nature?

Mary: By virgin you mean someone who never had sexual intercourse?

John: Last time I checked that was what the word means.

Mary: Suppose a doctor implants a fertilized egg in a woman who never had sexual intercourse. That would not violate any laws of nature, but it would lead to a virgin birth.

John: Yes, but I don't see the relevance of your example. You can't want to claim that Jesus' birth was a product of technology that didn't exist then.

Mary: Of course not. My point is that if a human agent, the doctor, can intervene and produce a virgin birth without violating any laws of nature, it seems strange to insist that God's intervention must violate a law of nature.

Brendan: You're going to have to explain a little more Mary. I don't follow what you're getting at.

Mary: I am saying that God could intervene in nature not by violating the laws of nature, but by changing the conditions to which the laws apply. Doctors do it all the time, but nobody claims that they are violating the laws of nature.

John: Are you saying that doctors are not part of nature?

Mary: I am saying that human agents often intervene in natural systems to change what would otherwise happen, without violating any laws of nature. If human agents can do it I don't see why a supernatural agent couldn't.

Brendan: Let's try a simpler example. Suppose we have a billiard table and I am about to make a shot. Newton's laws of motion tell us what will happen on the table. How could God change what will happen without violating those laws?

Mary: Suppose I were to move the balls around or introduced some additional balls just before you made your shot. Would that change what would have otherwise happened?

Brendan: Sure, but what is your point?

Mary: When I changed what would otherwise happen, was there any point in time at which Newton's laws of motion did not hold.

Brendan: No, but I still want to know what your point is.

Mary: My point is that I could intervene into that system without violating any laws of nature. All I had to do was change the conditions to which the laws apply. If God were to create some extra billiard balls on the table, or alter the position of the balls already on the table, he could intervene and change what would otherwise happen without violating any laws of nature.

John: I do not agree that Newton's laws of motion would not be broken. One of those laws, the third, is that for every action there is an equal and opposite reaction. The notion of God as unmoved mover violates that law.

Susan: I think that is too fast, John. Newton's laws of motion refer to the relation between physical objects. God is not a physical object and the relation between that which he creates or annihilates is not a physical relation. So I don't think your objection works.

Mary: What is true is that any new physical objects God creates will both act upon and be acted upon by previously existing physical objects. So, as I said before, Newton's laws apply, even though God changes the material conditions to which they apply.

Brendan: What if God annihilates a physical object. Does the law of action and reaction apply then?

Mary: I think that my argument still works. Newton's third law concerns the relation between two physical objects. If, due to God annihilating it, one of the objects no longer exists then there can be no relation between it and the other object, and thus there can be no question of Newton's third law being violated.

Holly: You people keep talking of God as he. Isn't that awfully anthropomorphic?

John: I agree. Why think of this hypothetical being as a he.

Susan: As president, I am going to rule that that is a discussion for another time. We need to keep on topic.

John: Mary has hands that she uses to throw the extra billiard ball onto the table. What is God going to use for hands.

Mary: Now who is being anthropomorphic? I do not think of God as having a body and needing to move things by his hands.

John: So he can move things simply by exercising his will?

Mary: Sure.

John: How is that analogous to your billiard example?

Mary: I would say that, by exercising my will, I can initiate a causal chain in my brain that leads eventually to me tossing an extra ball onto the billiard table, which alters what happens on the table without ever violating Newton's laws of motion. The difference between God and me is that my will can only act directly on a portion of my brain, whereas God, being infinitely powerful, can act directly on a billiard ball or can indeed create a billiard ball out of nothing.

Brendan: That seems to taken care of my billiard ball example, but what about a miracle like the virgin birth? How would it work?

Mary: Well if God created a spermatozoon at the right point and time in Mary's body, she could conceive while still a virgin.

Brendan: So what is unusual is not that Mary, once pregnant, would give birth, but that Mary becomes pregnant without any help from a human male?

Mary: Right. Barring any further supernatural intervention, Mary's pregnancy will be normal. The laws of nature will operate on whatever material conditions are the result of God's intervention.

Brendan: So if you take a miracle like the multiplication of the loaves and fishes, described in the New Testament, you're saying there is nothing unusual about those loaves and fishes. That doesn't seem right.

Mary: Well they are unusual in that they did not originate in the usual way, but they are not unusual in that once originated they will obey the laws of nature. Barring further intervention, the bread will go stale and the fishes will eventually spoil.

Brendan: I would like to say that this all sounds fishy, but that would be a bad pun. What I really want to know is whether your claim can be generalized.

Holly: Meaning what?

Susan: Meaning will it work for all miracles?

John: I don't think God exists or that miracles occur, but it seems to me that Mary's argument can be generalized. Physical events involve a certain amount and ordering of matter. If the event can be conceived then so can that particular amount and ordering of matter. So for any miracle it would be possible for God to produce it by bringing about that particular amount and ordering of matter.

Brendan: So, even though you do not think miracles ever take place, you agree that Mary is right that they should not be defined as involving violation of the laws of nature?

John: No, the argument has a certain appeal, but I don't think Mary is out of the woods as regards a miracle being a violation of the laws of nature. Let me explain.

Susan: I am sorry to interrupt, but our time is up for this meeting. We can continue the discussion next week. Right now, let me direct your attention to the wine and cheese that Professor Roberts has provided.

2

MIRACLES AND THE CONSERVATION OF ENERGY

Susan: Welcome everyone to our second meeting of the Socrates Society. As I mentioned at our previous meeting, we are devoting this term to philosophical discussion of the rationality of belief in miracles. I want to open this meeting by picking up from where our discussion ended last week.

In our previous meeting, John argued that a miracle should be defined as a violation of the laws of nature. Mary disagreed and suggested that, although miracles would involve supernatural intervention in nature, such intervention could take place without violating the laws of nature. Presumably God, by altering the material conditions to which the laws apply, could change what would otherwise happen without violating any laws of nature. An analogy she gave is that a person who tossed in an extra billiard ball could change what happened on a billiard table without violating Newton's laws of motion. John admitted that Mary's argument has some appeal, but claimed that a miracle must still violate at least one law of nature. We were just at the end of our time when John made this objection and we did not really get a chance to discuss it. It seems a good starting point for today's meeting.

Brendan: I found Mary's argument persuasive so I am interested in why John claims that on her account of a miracle a law of nature must still be violated.

John: Well if God starts creating extra billiard balls in the universe that doesn't seem consistent with the first law of thermodynamics.

Brendan: What is the first law of thermodynamics and why would God creating things be inconsistent with it?

John: It is what is known as the principle of the conservation of energy and it states that energy can neither be created nor destroyed. If we think of mass as a form of energy, creating billiard balls *ex nihilo* would be a violation of this law.

Holly: Kindly remember that I am not a philosophy major. What does *ex nihilo* mean?

Prof. Roberts: It's a Latin phrase meaning "out of nothing." Theists hold that the universe is not part of God and that he did not make it out of some preexisting stuff. Medieval philosophers coined the phrase to express this concept.

Brendan: What if God simply moves around already existing billiard balls instead of creating new ones?

John: That doesn't get around the problem. If a nonmaterial being, say God, causes something to move in a physical system that means there is more energy in the system than there was previously and that is going to violate the principle of the conservation of energy.

Holly: What if God is energy?

Prof. Roberts: I don't think that will work. Remember what I said about the term "ex nihilo." Saying that God is energy would suggest that the universe is part of God and that is something the theist denies. It would also seem to suggest that God is somehow material rather than nonmaterial.

Holly: Why would it suggest that God is material?

Prof. Roberts: Energy is conceived as a property of material systems. To suggest that God is energy would mean that we have to think of God either as a material system or the property of a material system.

Brendan: What do you say to John's objection Mary? It looks like your claim that miracles do not violate any laws of nature is in trouble.

Mary: I'm not quite sure what to say. I think there must be something wrong with John's argument, but I can't say what it is at the moment.

Susan: John, while Mary tries to figure out what she thinks is wrong with your argument, could you go into a little more detail why you think God's intervention in nature would violate the principle of the conservation of energy. I want to be sure I understand what the problem is.

John: I'll try. Suppose God causes a billiard ball to move.

Susan: Ok. Go on.

John: That billiard ball now has kinetic energy.

Susan: So far, so good, I follow.

John: But if that billiard ball was not caused to move by some physical cause, but rather by the direct influence of God, the kinetic energy of the billiard ball was not transferred from some material source. That means there is more energy in the universe than previously. If the amount of energy in the universe is not conserved that violates the principle of the conservation of energy.

Susan: What if God simply creates a billiard ball?

John: Physicists treat mass as a form of energy. If God creates a billiard ball this also violates the principle of the conservation of energy, since it implies that the amount of energy in the universe is not constant.

Susan: What if every time God creates energy in one place, he destroys an equal amount in another? That wouldn't violate the principle would it?

John: Yes it would. The principle states that energy can neither be created nor destroyed; that the total amount of energy in the universe would remain the same does not negate that, on such a hypothesis, energy would still be created and destroyed. It would just mean that God is creating and destroying energy in equal amounts.

Mary: John, you said that physicists treat mass as just a form of energy and hold that the universe is composed of different forms of energy.

John: Yes, I would agree with that.

Mary: So if energy can neither be created nor destroyed the universe must always have existed and nothing could have made it and nothing can destroy it. That is not only going to rule out miracles, it's going to rule out the claim that God created the universe.

Brendan: Slow down Mary. Why do you say that?

Mary: Well if energy can neither be created nor destroyed and the universe is composed of various forms of energy, God could not have created the universe. It sounds as if John is saying that one can't believe in the principle of the conservation of energy and still be a theist.

John: I hadn't thought quite that far ahead, but yes, if an essential claim of theism is that God created the universe, then I don't think you can accept the principle of the conservation of energy and still be a theist. You're going to have to choose between science and belief in God and I know which one I'm going for. There's far more evidence for the principle than there is for God.

Susan: But aren't there lots of scientists that accept the principle and still believe in God? Doesn't that suggest you're wrong?

John: Not really. Lots of people hold contradictory beliefs, but don't realize it.

Holly: That sounds a bit pretentious on your part.

John: Why do you say that? I'm just going where the argument takes me.

Mary: I wonder if you would say that if the argument looked like it was taking you towards theism. And it does seem to be claiming a lot to suggest that you can't do science and believe in God.

John: Well it was you who pointed out that the principle of the conservation of energy, which is a basic law of nature if ever there was one, is inconsistent with the idea of the universe being created by God. As I said, I'm just going where the argument takes me.

Susan: Let us try to stick with the argument and leave personal motivations out of the discussion.

Brendan: I am not sure that is possible.

Susan: I agree, but let us at least try.

Prof. Roberts: Perhaps it would be helpful to examine the principle of the conservation of energy a little more closely. John, what do you take the principle to claim?

John: I think I have made that clear, but here goes. Although its form may change, energy can neither be created nor destroyed.

Susan: I always thought of the principle as the claim that energy is conserved in an isolated system.

John: Yes, but it is the same claim.

Brendan: So the claim "Energy can neither be created nor destroyed" is equivalent to the claim "In an isolated system energy is conserved"?

John: Yes. If it is true that energy can neither be created nor destroyed, then it has to be true that in an isolated system energy is conserved.

Prof. Roberts: Careful John. It may be that if the claim that energy can neither be created nor destroyed is true, then the claim that in an isolated system energy is conserved must be true, but that doesn't guarantee the two statements are equivalent.

John: Why not?

Prof. Roberts: Well, the fact that I am a human father guarantees that I am a human male, but it would be wrong to conclude that being a human male is equivalent to being a human father. The claim that "energy can neither be created nor destroyed" and the claim that "in an isolated system energy is conserved" will only be equivalent if each guarantees the truth of the other.

Brendan: I get it. We not only have to ask whether the truth of the claim energy can neither be created nor destroyed guarantees the truth of the claim that in an isolated system energy is conserved, but whether the truth of the claim energy is conserved in an isolated system guarantees the truth of the claim that energy can neither be created nor destroyed.

Susan: Could you put that a little more simply?

Brendan: How about this? If it is possible that the claim "In an isolated system energy is conserved" is true but the claim "Energy can neither be created nor destroyed" is false, then the two claims do not say exactly the same thing and thus are not equivalent.

Holly: But didn't we just say that if it is true that energy can neither be created nor destroyed then it must be true that in an isolated system energy is conserved?

Brendan: Sure, but that doesn't mean they say the same thing. You cannot assume that because energy is conserved in an isolated system it must be true that it cannot be created or destroyed, just as you cannot assume that because someone is a human male he is a father.

Holly: Ok, we have two forms of the principle of the conservation of energy that don't quite say the same thing. So what? How does that get around John's claim that God performing a miracle violates the principle?

Susan: Mary, you've been pretty silent. Are you ready to accept John's claim that miracles would violate the principle of the conservation of energy?

Mary: I agree that miracles would require that the claim that energy can neither be created nor destroyed is false, but no theist could agree with that claim anyway, since it rules out not only miracles, but God's creation of the universe.

John: So you admit that miracles would violate the principle?

Mary: Only if the principle of the conservation of energy is taken to claim that energy can neither be created nor destroyed. If the principle is taken to claim that energy is conserved in an isolated system then I don't think miracles would violate it.

John: How can you say that? You have admitted that God performing a miracle would change the amount of energy in the universe. That means energy would not be conserved and that violates the principle.

Mary: No it doesn't. I agree that energy is conserved in an isolated system, but that tells us nothing about whether in fact the universe is an isolated system. A miracle would not falsify the claim that energy is conserved in an isolated system, but rather the claim that the universe is an isolated system.

Holly: So you're not denying that it is true that energy is conserved in an isolated system?

Mary: No. I am denying that we can assume the universe is an isolated system. If God exists and performs a miracle, then the universe cannot be considered an isolated system.

John: So if God introduces some extra mass/energy into the universe—say by multiplying some loaves and fishes—this doesn't violate the principle of the conservation of energy?

Mary: Not if by the principle you mean the claim that energy is conserved in an isolated system. What it would demonstrate is that the universe is not an isolated system, but is open to the causal influence of God. To claim that energy is conserved in an isolated system tells us nothing about whether in fact a particular system is in fact isolated.

Brendan: I am not sure that I agree that a miracle would not violate the claim that energy is conserved in an isolated system. Suppose we define an isolated system as one into which neither energy nor matter is transferred. Wouldn't it follow that a miracle, at least as you are defining it, would be inconsistent not only with the claim that energy can neither be created nor destroyed, but with the claim that energy is conserved in an isolated system?

Mary: Would you agree that by isolated system, we mean a system that is not causally affected by something other than itself?

Brendan: Yes, I agree with that.

Mary: Then I disagree that an isolated system can be defined as one into which neither energy nor matter is transferred.

Brendan: Why not?

Mary: Well, unless we assume that energy can neither be created nor destroyed, there is no reason to think that a system into which neither energy nor matter has been transferred is causally isolated. If God creates or annihilates energy or matter within a system, we would have a system into which neither energy nor matter had been transferred, but which could not accurately be described as isolated. Such an action by God is inconsistent with the claim that energy can neither be created nor destroyed, but not with the claim that energy is conserved in an isolated system.

Brendan: But don't scientists typically assume that a system into which there has been no transfer of energy is in fact isolated?

Mary: Yes, but that is only because they do not take into account the possibility of God acting. Once we take into account the possibility of God creating energy or matter within a system it becomes clear you can't define an isolated system as one into which neither energy nor matter is transferred.

John: You could if God does not exist.

Mary: But you cannot simply assume that God does not exist. My point is that if God does exist and does perform a miracle by creating energy or matter within a particular system such action does not falsify the claim that energy is conserved in an isolated system, since such a system is not isolated, but is acted on by God.

Brendan: What would scientists give as an example of an isolated system. And don't say a system in which there has been no transfer of energy.

John: I do not think there are any, except the universe. All systems within the universe are affected by something external to them. Only the universe is a completely isolated system in the sense that there is nothing external to it that can causally affect it.

Mary: You cannot just assume that the universe is all that exists and that there is, therefore, nothing that can causally affect it. You are begging the question of God's existence. If God exists then the universe is not an isolated system, since it could causally be affected by God, its creator.

Holly: Just to be sure I understand, what do philosophers mean by the term "begging the question"?

Susan: In popular usage, the term means simply to raise a question. In philosophical usage, it means that you are taking for granted something you should be arguing for.

Holly: How about an example?

Susan: A lot, though not all, circular arguments are question begging. There used to be a comedy skit where three thieves are dividing up four jewels. The one thief gives a jewel to each of his fellow thieves and keeps two for himself. When they question him why he gets two jewels and they only get one, he answers that it is because he is the leader. They then ask why he is the leader and he answers that it is because he has two jewels and they only have one.

Holly: Thanks, I get it. That thief never really justifies why he should be the leader and get two jewels. Philosophically speaking, you beg the question when you take a claim as justified, when really you have not provided any reason to accept it.

Prof. Roberts: Nicely put Holly. I think you would do well in philosophy classes.

John: Getting back to our discussion, I'll admit that if God exists the universe is not an isolated system, but do you really want to claim that the principle of the conservation of energy is a law that has no application. It appears that, according to theists, there are no causally isolated systems.

Mary: Well, if as theists hold, the universe depends for its existence upon God, it makes no sense to claim that it is isolated. However, I do not claim that the principle of the conservation has no application. It tells us that, to the degree that a system is isolated, in the sense that it is not affected by something external to it, its energy is conserved. Scientists make claims about how an ideal gas would behave or what would happen on a frictionless surface, even though there are no ideal gases or totally frictionless surfaces. So I do not see why the claim that energy is conserved in an isolated system should be treated any differently. The principle is in some sense ideal, but it is not vacuous.

Holly: If it were vacuous it would not tell us anything.

Mary: Right. It tells us quite a lot, even if there are, in fact, no completely isolated systems.

Brendan: So we have two versions of the principle of the conservation of energy. One version, the claim that energy can neither be created nor destroyed would be violated by God performing a miracle; the other version, the claim that energy is conserved in an isolated system would not be violated by God performing a miracle. Where do we go from here? Does one just get to pick which version you like best?

John: I'm going with the version that states energy can neither be created nor destroyed.

Mary: I wonder whether you are going where the argument takes you or are you taking the argument where you want to go? I hope you have a better reason than that it is the version of the principle that rules out miracles.

Brendan: I suppose that you, Mary, are going with the version of the principle that states energy is conserved in an isolated system?

Mary: That's what I want to say, but I would like to be able to have a good reason for rejecting John's claim that energy can neither be created nor destroyed. It is not enough to reject it just on the basis that I don't like the fact that it rules out theism.

Prof. Roberts: Maybe you should think further about the relation between the two versions of the principle. We have seen that they are not equivalent, but they are related.

Holly: What do you mean?

Prof. Roberts: As we noted earlier, being a human father guarantees that you are a human male, but being a human male does not guarantee that you are a human father. There is a logical relation between the two claims, even if it is not one of equivalency.

Susan: Ok. So if it is true that energy can neither be created nor destroyed, that guarantees that energy is conserved in an isolated system.

John (interrupting): That's right.

Susan: Let me finish. But if it is true that energy is conserved in an isolated system that does not guarantee that energy can neither be created nor destroyed.

Mary: I like where this is going.

Holly: But how does this help answer Brendan's question of which version of the principle to accept?

Prof. Roberts: Why do you accept the principle of the conservation of energy as a law of nature.

John: That's easy. There is an enormous amount of scientific evidence in its favor.

Prof. Roberts: Does that scientific evidence equally support each version of the principle?

Brendan: What are you getting at?

Mary: I think I understand Prof. Roberts's point. Evidence for someone being a father is evidence that the person is a male, but evidence for someone being a human male is not evidence that the person is a human father. So evidence that energy cannot be created or destroyed would be evidence that energy is conserved in an isolated system, but evidence that energy is conserved in an isolated system is not evidence that energy cannot be created or destroyed.

Susan: So if the scientific evidence establishes that energy can neither be created nor destroyed then it also establishes that energy is conserved in an isolated system, but if it establishes that energy is conserved in an isolated system then it does not establish that energy can neither be created nor destroyed.

Brendan: So what is the verdict? What does the scientific evidence establish?

Mary: All that any experiment could establish is that to the degree that a system is isolated, energy is conserved. It looks like my version of the principle is the one supported by the scientific evidence. And that is the version that would not be violated by God performing a miracle.

John: Not so fast. Evidence that someone is a male is not evidence against his being a father. The fact that the scientific evidence establishes Mary's claim that energy is conserved in an isolated system, rather than my claim that energy can neither be created or destroyed, doesn't disestablish my claim. It could still be true that energy can neither be created nor destroyed.

Susan: But what is your evidence that it is true that energy can neither be created nor destroyed?

John: If energy can neither be created or destroyed that explains why energy is conserved in an isolated system. Further, given there is no evidence that energy is ever created or destroyed, I think we are entitled to say it can't be created or destroyed.

Mary: I don't think those are good reasons to accept the claim that energy can neither be created nor destroyed. First, God's creation of a physical universe in which cause and effect operate equally explains why energy is conserved in an isolated system. Second, your claim that there is no evidence that energy is ever created or destroyed simply assumes that miracles—which you earlier insisted would involve the creation of energy—never happen. You are begging the question again. You can't justify the claim that energy can neither be created nor destroyed on the assumption that it never has been created or destroyed, and then turn around and reject miracles on the basis that they would involve the creation or destruction of energy. That's a vicious circle.

Susan: I didn't quite follow that last bit, Mary.

Mary: If John's reason for accepting that energy can neither be created or destroyed is that there is no evidence it has been created or destroyed, he cannot then use the claim that energy can neither be created nor destroyed as a basis for rejecting evidence which suggests that it can be created or destroyed.

Susan: So, if miracles involve the creation or destruction of energy, and John's only reason for believing that energy can neither be created nor destroyed is that there is no evidence that energy is created or destroyed, he is not entitled to ignore reports of miracles, since if they occur they are evidence that energy is created or destroyed?

Mary: Right. Here is an analogy. If my only reason for believing there are no mice in the building is that nobody has seen any, then if I get reports of mice being seen I cannot reject those reports on the grounds that I have already established that there are no mice around.

John: But you cannot simply assume that miracles do occur. Do not accuse me of begging questions and then turn around and do it yourself.

Mary: I am not begging the question of whether miracles occur. What I am asserting is that you cannot use the claim that energy can neither be created nor destroyed as a basis for rejecting claims that miracles happen. If they occur they are good evidence that, although energy is conserved in an isolated system, it is false that energy can neither be created nor destroyed.

John: That's a very big if. Other than highly questionable, superstitious accounts of miracles is there any actual evidence that energy can be created or destroyed?

Brendan: That's not fair, John. We haven't established that accounts of miracle are questionable or superstitious.

Mary: It seems to me that all you have going for your claim that energy cannot be created or destroyed is a presumed lack of evidence against it. I can, at least in principle, appeal to positive testimonial evidence in favor of miracles. You claim that you want to go where the evidence leads, but now you refuse to take it seriously.

John: If there was any serious evidence I would take it seriously.

Mary: I cannot help thinking you have already made up your mind before looking at any potential evidence.

Susan: Remember we said that we were going to keep things friendly.

Brendan: I want to pick up on John's question of whether there is actual evidence that energy can be created or destroyed. Over the weekend, I was looking at a book about the big bang theory in cosmology. If I understand it correctly, most cosmologists think there was an absolute beginning to the physical universe. If the universe is composed of mass/energy wouldn't that mean there was an absolute beginning to that mass/energy?

John: I suppose so, but what is your point.

Brendan: If mass/energy can have an absolute beginning, isn't that inconsistent with the claim that energy cannot be created or destroyed? How could something that cannot be created have a beginning? It looks like the big bang theory is consistent with the claim that energy is conserved in an isolated system, but inconsistent with the claim that energy can neither be created nor destroyed.

Mary: So it looks as if within established science there are good reasons to reject the claim that energy can neither be created nor destroyed.

Brendan: Looks like it.

John: I am not willing to say that the big bang theory constitutes established science.

Brendan: From what I have read cosmologists think they have a lot of evidence that supports it.

Mary: So it looks like evidence for the big bang theory is evidence that energy can be created. Quite apart from the issue of miracle that means your claim, John, that there is no evidence that energy can be created or destroyed is false.

John: Ok, it seems that if I want to talk about the principle of the conservation of energy as a well-evidenced law of nature that I will have to go with the version that holds that energy is conserved in an isolated system. I admit that the evidence for this form of the principle does not necessarily justify the further claim that energy can neither be created nor destroyed.

Mary: And that means you can't claim that a miracle would involve violating the principle of the conservation of energy.

John: I guess not.

Susan: So you agree with Mary that a miracle could occur without violating any laws of nature?

John: Yes, but I want to emphasize that nothing that has been said demonstrates that miracles do in fact occur. All that I have agreed to is that if they do occur they need not violate the laws of nature.

Mary: You're right, but so far we are only discussing how miracles should be defined, not whether there is good evidence they actually occur. That is a different question.

John: I suggest you read David Hume's "Of Miracles" if you want the answer to that question. No offense Mary, but I think he conclusively demonstrates that belief in miracles can never be rational.

Susan: Good discussion, but once again we are out of time. I think John's suggestion that we read Hume's "Of Miracles" is a good one. Let us do that in preparation for next week's meeting.

3

HUME'S A PRIORI ARGUMENT

Susan: Welcome people. For our third meeting we have agreed to look at David Hume's famous discussion of miracles found in the tenth chapter of his book *An Enquiry Concerning Human Understanding*. Who wants to start the discussion.

John: I said last meeting that Hume demonstrates the impossibility of establishing a rational belief in miracles. When I reread "Of Miracles" for today's meeting I was more convinced than ever.

Prof. Roberts: What do you take Hume's argument to be John?

John: I'm glad you asked that Professor. The argument I have in mind is the one that Hume develops in part 1 of his essay "Of Miracles." I took the time to write out the argument in Hume's own words, since I didn't want people telling me I had got it wrong. Here it is:[1]

1. "Experience [is] our only guide in reasoning concerning matters of fact."

---

1. Hume, *Enquiry Concerning Human Understanding*, 144–48.

2. "It must be acknowledged that this guide [experience] is not altogether infallible but in some cases is apt to lead us into errors."

3. "A wise man, therefore, proportions his belief to the evidence. In such conclusions as are founded on an infallible experience, he expects the event with the last degree of assurance, and regards his past experience as a full *proof* of the future existence of that event. In other cases, he proceeds with more caution: He weighs the opposite experiments: He considers which side is supported by the greater number of experiments: to that side he inclines, with doubt and hesitation; and when at last he fixes his judgement, the evidence exceeds not what we properly call *probability*."

4. "It is evident that we ought not to make an exception to this maxim in favour of human testimony, whose connexion with any event seems, in itself, as little necessary as any other."

5. "A miracle is a violation of the laws of nature."

6. Since "a firm and unalterable experience has established these laws, the proof against a miracle, from the very nature of the fact, is as entire as any argument from experience can possibly be imagined."

7. Thus there is "a direct and full *proof*, from the nature of the fact, against the existence of any miracle; nor can such a proof be destroyed, or the miracle rendered credible, but by an opposite proof, which is superior."

8. Therefore "no testimony is sufficient to establish a miracle, unless the testimony be of such a kind, that its falsehood would be more miraculous, than the fact, which it endeavours to establish; and even in that case there is a mutual destruction of arguments, and the superior only gives us an assurance suitable to that degree of force which remains, after deducting the inferior."

Holly: Do you think he meant to claim there could never be enough evidence to justify believing in a miracle or only that you would need a lot of evidence?

John: I think he meant there could never, even in principle, be enough evidence to justify belief.

Brendan: But Hume never quite comes out and says that, does he?

John: He doesn't have to. If the proof against a miracle "is as entire as any argument from experience can possibly be imagined" and a miracle can only be rendered credible "by an opposite proof, which is superior" there is no way belief in a miracle can ever be justified, since there is no way the superior proof he requires is possible.

Holly: Why not?

John: Because he just said the proof against a miracle was as great as could possibly be imagined. That means we cannot even imagine the evidence for a miracle outweighing the evidence against it. There is no way, even in theory, that one could trump a proof against miracle which "is as entire as any argument from experience can possibly be imagined."

Mary: So it is as if Hume is saying to the believer, "I will accept the occurrence of a miracle if you give me enough evidence for it, but, of course you should realize it is impossible that there is ever enough evidence for one."

John: Yes, Hume by all accounts was very fond of irony.

Brendan: You make a good case, but you are talking about the argument of part 1. If you are right in suggesting that Hume intended to claim that his argument totally ruled out the possibility of belief in miracles, why part 2 and the arguments we find there.

John: Hume must have known that there would be people who would not accept the argument in part 1. I think he wanted to say to them that even if they did not accept that it is impossible there could ever be enough evidence to justify belief in miracles, they should realize that the evidence for miracles is very poor and does not even come close to what is needed. I think he wants to make the point the actual evidence supporting belief in miracles is more worthy of ridicule than serious discussion. Certainly, whatever the explanation of part 2 is, there are several places in it where Hume presupposes the argument of part 1 as demonstrating the impossibility of rational belief in miracles.

Brendan: For instance.

John: Perhaps the best example is where, after suggesting the evidence for reported miracles associated with a Roman Catholic sect known as the Jansenists, is extremely good, Hume writes, "What have we to oppose to such a cloud of witnesses, but the absolute impossibility or miraculous nature of the events, which they relate? And this surely, in the eyes of all reasonable people, will alone be regarded as a sufficient refutation."[2] A further example is where he claims that those who are wise and learned are justified in deriding a report of a miracle as absurd, "without informing themselves of the particular facts by which it may be distinctly refuted."[3] It seems pretty clear that in Hume's view the fact that a reported event is a miracle makes rational justification of belief in its occurrence impossible and that detailed examination of apparent evidence in its favor is, therefore, unnecessary. Unless we take him as simply being dogmatic, he must be taken as claiming that his argument of part 1 justifies this conclusion.

Brendan: I concede that John makes a good case, though I would like a little better explanation of part 2 than he gives. Too bad we cannot ask Hume in person what he intended to claim in the argument of part 1.

Prof. Roberts: We cannot ask Hume directly, but in addition to the points that John made it should be added that all Hume's early critics assumed that Hume intended to demonstrate the impossibility of there ever existing sufficient evidence to justify belief

---

2. Hume, *Enquiry Concerning Human Understanding*, 157–58.
3. Ibid., 153.

in miracles. Hume, in replying to their criticisms, never suggested that they had misinterpreted what he intended to claim.[4] It is hard to believe that if these early critics fundamentally misunderstood the purpose of his argument, that Hume would have remained silent on so important a point.

Susan: Isn't that an argument from silence Prof. Roberts? When I took informal logic from you two years ago, you said that such arguments are often not very strong. You told us that just because someone does not mention that she holds a certain view cannot automatically be taken to mean that she does not hold that view.

Prof. Roberts: I did, but I also said that not all arguments from silence are weak. An argument from silence is weak if there is no good reason to expect that a view that is not mentioned would have been mentioned if the person held that view. For example, there is no good reason to think that in my lectures I would mention the fact that I believe that Bobby Fischer was one of the greatest chess players of all time, so my failure to mention that I do in fact believe this is not a good reason to conclude that I do not hold this view. In this case, however, it is very reasonable to believe that Hume would have responded to any fundamental misreading of an argument he was extremely proud of. So his not mentioning that he thought his critics were misunderstanding what he wanted to claim regarding belief in miracles is strong evidence that he did hold the view they were attributing to him.

Mary: Hume seems exclusively concerned with evaluating reports of miracles. Does he ever consider the possibility of whether a person might directly observe a miracle.

Prof. Roberts: You are right Mary. He confines himself to the evaluation of testimony.

Mary: Why do you think that is?

Prof. Roberts: Probably, for two reasons. The first is that Hume was wanting to undermine the Christian apologists of his

4. Burns, *Great Debate on Miracles*, 153.

day who claimed that it was reasonable to believe in Christianity on the basis of Christ's miracles and that these miracles could be accepted on the basis of the testimony of the writers of Scripture. Demonstrating the impossibility of testimonial evidence ever being sufficient to justify belief in a miracle would totally undermine those apologists. The second, I suspect, is that Hume dismissed the possibility of personally experiencing a miracle.

Holly: So Hume is arguing that miracles are impossible?

Prof. Roberts: Well there are some places where he seems to say that, but a more charitable reading is not that he claims to have demonstrated that miracles cannot occur, but rather that one could never be justified in believing in their occurrence on the basis of testimony.

John: I agree with Prof. Roberts. I think this argument must have appealed to Hume's love of irony. He doesn't for a moment on the personal level believe that miracles really occur, but he is not going to deny the believer that possibility, only the possibility that one could ever be rationally justified in believing they occur.

Susan: We seem to have arrived at some sort of consensus on how the argument of part 1 should be read. Establishing this, however, is only a preliminary to asking if the argument is a good one.

John: I think it is a simple and elegant demonstration of why belief in miracles can never be rational.

Mary: I have been wondering if maybe the argument proves too much.

Brendan: What do you mean, "proves too much"?

Mary: A miracle is an unusual event that has a supernatural cause, but there can also be unusual events that have natural causes. Won't Hume's argument also rule out this latter type of unusual event?

Brendan: I need more explanation of what you take to be the problem.

Mary: Hume's argument seems not only to rule out accepting reports of miracles, but any unusual event that is outside one's personal experience.

Brendan: I still don't see the problem.

Mary: Apart from the fact that one's personal experience can be pretty limited, it is hard to see how science will go forward if every time scientists get a report of an unusual event that runs counter to what they expect they are, to use Hume's words "contented, in general, to deride its absurdity, without informing themselves of the particular facts, by which it may be refuted."[5]

John: I don't think you're being fair to Hume, Mary. He distinguishes between marvels and miracles. A marvel is an unusual event with a natural but unknown cause, a miracle is an unusual event with a supernatural cause. Unlike miracles, belief in marvels can be justified if there is strong enough testimonial evidence in their favor.

Brendan: Why does Hume think that belief in marvels can be justified on the basis of testimony, but miracles cannot.

John: A marvel may be unexpected, but it is not contrary to our experience, since it happens under conditions of which we have no experience. That is the point of Hume's Indian prince example. The Indian prince, living in a warm climate, had no experience of water's behavior under extremely cold conditions and thus reports that it becomes solid enough to walk on under those conditions were not really contrary to his experience. As Hume puts it, "the inhabitants of Sumatra have always seen water fluid in their own climate . . . but they never saw water in Muscovy during the winter; and therefore they cannot reasonably be positive what would there be the consequence."[6]

Mary: You still haven't explained why testimony can be sufficient to establish a marvel, but not a miracle.

5. Burns, *Great Debate on Miracles*, 153.
6. Ibid., 148.

John: A miracle, unlike a marvel, is contrary to our experience in that it is claimed to occur, to use Hume's words, "in cases where all the circumstances are the same."[7]

Mary: I don't think that is going to work.

John: Why not?

Mary: No believer is going to say that miracles "are contrary to uniform experience of the course of nature in cases where all the circumstances are the same." Miracles occur when the circumstances are not all the same— namely, when God intervenes and causes something different to happen. When I claim that the virgin birth occurred, I am claiming that there was an extra causal factor involved that is not present in usual cases of conception.

John: But your positing that extra causal factor seems based on first accepting the report of the miracle. That is not true of the Indian prince example. He could point to something different in the background conditions that suggested a causal factor foreign to his experience might be at work.

Mary: That is true in the case of the Indian prince, but there are many cases where the different circumstance is not immediately obvious and comes only after accepting the reported phenomena.

John: I presume you can point to some examples.

Mary: I think there are lots, but meteorites are a good one. Most people do not personally experience stones falling out of a clear sky. LaPlace, the famous French astronomer, and his fellow scientists refused to accept testimony that this sometimes happened, on the basis that they could point to no circumstance contrary to their ordinary experience that would explain the phenomena. That kind of dogmatism on their part did not further scientific discovery. In fact, it was the clergy of the day, not the scientists, who insisted that reports of meteors be taken seriously.[8]

Brendan: So your point is?

7. Ibid., 147–48.

8. Jaki, *Miracles and Physics*, 99.

Mary: Hume is wrong when he claims that believers hold that miracles are contrary to the usual course of nature where all the causal factors are the same. Also, it is a mistake to claim that in the case of unusual events with a presumed natural but unknown cause, one can always point to something different in the background circumstances that justifies accepting the existence of such events on the basis of testimony.

Brendan: I think you need to explain a little further.

Mary: I am making two points. First, the distinction Hume draws between a marvel and a miracle does not really hold up, since believers do not define a miracle as an event that is "contrary to uniform experience of the course of nature in cases where all the circumstances are the same." A more plausible way of making the distinction would be to say that a marvel is an unusual event with a natural cause and that a miracle is an unusual event with a supernatural cause. Second, making this distinction does not let Hume escape the charge that his argument proves too much, since often it is only by accepting the existence of the "marvel" on the basis of what is considered reliable testimony, that scientists conduct the investigation that uncovers its cause.

Susan: Something else bothers me about the argument. We agreed that Hume is best understood not as claiming that miracles can't occur, but rather as claiming that one can never have enough evidence to justify belief in their occurrence. It seems strange to claim that miracles may be possible, but that one should never believe in them no matter how excellent the evidence.

John: We also said that Hume is only talking about testimonial evidence. He never claims you couldn't believe in a miracle if you actually saw one.

Mary: Even supposing that Hume would say that belief in a miracle can be justified if one actually observes it, I think that he is way too skeptical of testimony.

John: Why? Do you have a different objection than the one you just raised concerning the argument proving too much? I think Hume is off the hook if he acknowledges that one could be justified in believing in a miracle if one actually experienced one first hand, but sticks to his argument that one could never be justified in believing in a miracle on the basis of testimony.

Mary: I do not think he is off the hook at all. It seems strange to say that if I were actually to observe a miracle then I would be justified in believing it occurred, but that I would still have to reject all reports of miracles. That commits me to saying that although it could be rational to believe that I observed a miracle it could never be rational to believe that others observed a miracle. What if I were not the only person to witness the miracle? Does that mean that I would be justified in believing that it occurred, but that I would have to think that other people who claimed to have witnessed it are either lying or deceived?

Brendan: You need to explain that one a little better Mary. I am not quite following your argument.

Mary: Well if, according to Hume argument, I should always disbelieve reports of miracles then I should reject as absurd the other witnesses' claims that the miracle occurred. On the basis of my own experience, however, I am justified in believing that it did occur. So if I were to be present at a miracle, say Jesus walking on water, I would be entitled to believe on the basis of my experience that Jesus did walk on water, but I would have to disbelieve others who were present when they report having seen the same event. That commits me to claiming that it is both rational and irrational to believe the miracle occurred. That does not make any sense. If there are circumstances under which it would be rational for me to think that I had observed a miracle then there must be circumstances under which it is rational to think someone else has observed a miracle.

Brendan: Couldn't we say that you are justified in believing others to have observed a miracle only if you observed the same miracle?

Mary: That seems to be requiring too much. Why wouldn't I think that at least some other people can be as reliable an observer as me? Why is it only rational to believe their reports if I have witnessed the event myself?

Susan: Mary's example of meteors is a good one. I have never observed stones falling out of the sky, but I think it is rational to believe other peoples' reports of this.

Brendan: I'd like to hear from John. Susan and Mary have raised a couple of interesting objections. Do you still think, to use your words, that "the argument is a simple and elegant demonstration of why belief in miracles can never be rational"?

John: I admit that the issue is not as simple as I first suggested, but I think Hume's argument is fundamentally correct, even if it needs a little fine tuning here and there. It demonstrates that there is always a conflict between our evidence for the laws of nature and the testimony for a miracle. Further, short of actually experiencing a miracle, it seems there is always going to be more evidence for the laws of nature than there is for a miracle.

Brendan: I think it may take a little more than "fine tuning" to deal with the objections Mary has raised.

Prof. Roberts: If I can interject, I think it is important that in evaluating Hume's argument you take into account your earlier discussion concerning whether miracles should be thought of as violations of the laws of nature.

Brendan: What are you getting at Professor?

Prof. Roberts: Maybe instead of debating whether the evidence for a miracle can ever outweigh the evidence for the laws of nature, you ought to ask whether it is true that the evidence for a miracle necessarily conflicts with the evidence for the laws of nature.

Holly: I'll bite. Is it true that the evidence for a miracle has to conflict with the evidence for the laws of nature?

John: It's clear that Hume thought so. The crucial point of his argument is that the evidence for the laws of nature is evidence against the occurrence of miracles and must outweigh any body of testimonial evidence for miracles.

Prof. Roberts: But why did Hume think this?

Brendan: As we saw, it was because he defined miracles as violations of laws of nature.

Susan: I think I get your point Professor. If miracles need not involve violations of the laws of nature then the evidence for a miracle does not necessarily conflict with the evidence for the laws of nature.

Brendan: And in our earlier discussion we arrived at the conclusion that miracles should not be thought of as violating the laws of nature.

Mary: That means that Hume's argument cannot get started, since it depends on there being a conflict between the evidence for the laws of nature and the evidence for miracles, and there is no such conflict.

Holly: Slow down and explain things a little more. As I have mentioned several times before, not everyone here is a philosophy major.

Mary: Hume's argument is what is known as a "balance of probabilities" argument. He wants to say that one cannot accept both miracles and the laws of nature.

Holly: Sorry to interrupt, but is that because according to Hume miracles have to be defined as violations of the laws of nature?

Mary: Yes. So given that you cannot believe in both miracles and the laws of nature, Hume says that you should believe that for which there is the most evidence. He then goes on to say that, from the very nature of the case, there must always be more evidence for the laws of nature than for a miracle report.

Holly: Why is that?

Mary: He presumes that none of us have ever personally experienced a miracle, that is to say a violation of the laws of nature. That means we have what he calls a uniform experience that the laws of nature are without any exceptions. We do not have, however, a uniform experience of people always telling the truth or not being mistaken. There must always, therefore, be more evidence for the laws of nature than there is for miracles and thus testimony must always be insufficient to justify belief in a miracle.

Brendan: But if miracles need not be defined as violating the laws of nature there is no reason to think that the evidence for the laws of nature must conflict with the evidence for miracles.

Mary: And that means that Hume's argument cannot get started, since it depends on viewing the two bodies of evidence as being in conflict.

John: Technically, you may be right that miracles would not violate the laws of nature, but I think Hume's more fundamental point still holds.

Brendan: That point being what?

John: The point being that belief in miracles is at odds with a scientific view of reality.

Brendan: Why do you say that?

John: Science is the search for the natural causes of physical events. When you claim an event is a miracle you are claiming it has a supernatural cause. How can that be consistent with a scientific view of reality?

Mary: Searching for natural causes is not the same as always finding them.

John: But if you are going to be scientific you have to assume they exist.

Mary: Why can't you simply assume natural causes might exist. Even if I agree that science is the search for natural causes, how scientific is it to insist in advance of actually investigating that all events have in fact natural causes?

Susan: I'm with Mary on this one. When John proposes that we have to hold that all events have natural causes, it sounds more like metaphysics than science.

John: I was proposing a methodology, not a metaphysic. I did not say that all events actually have natural causes, only that as scientists we have to assume they do.

Mary: You keep asserting that assumption is necessary, but you still have not explained why scientists cannot search for natural causes without having to insist that they must always exist.

John: Science has to proceed on the assumption that it can give a complete account of the world in terms of natural causes.

Mary: Are you not just using different words to say the same thing? Why is that a necessary assumption of science? If I want to investigate whether there is life on Venus I only have to be open to the possibility that it exists, I do not have to assume that it does in fact exist, or even that it probably exists.

Prof. Roberts: The discussion has taken an interesting direction, but we seem to have strayed from directly considering Hume's argument. I suggest that you come back to this issue after you finish looking at Hume. You still have the arguments of part 2 of Hume's essay to discuss.

Brendan: So what do we want to say about the argument of part 1 before we move to discussing part 2?

Susan: Summarized, the argument of part 1 depends on defining miracles as violations of the laws of nature and thus viewing any evidence for the laws of nature as evidence against miracles. This allows Hume to argue that, since the evidence for the laws of nature is always greater than the evidence for miracles, belief in miracles can never be justified.

Mary: As regards criticisms, we noted three. First, the argument seems not only to rule out belief in miracles, but accepting reports of unusual natural events. Second, it seems to lead to the conclusion that even if one were to witness a miracle one could not believe the reports of others who witnessed the same event. Third, the argument cannot get started unless miracles are incorrectly defined as violations of the laws of nature.

Susan: That last criticism seems to be pretty important. If the evidence for a miracle does not necessarily conflict with the evidence for the laws of nature then the burden of proof seems to be on the sceptic to explain why we should not believe in miracles.

Holly: Once again, I need you to explain in a little more detail. Why do you say that?

Susan: In the absence of conflicting evidence or reason to believe that the testimony in question is unreliable we tend to believe what people claim to have observed. The point of Hume's argument was to claim that there was a necessary conflict between the evidence for the laws of nature and testimonial evidence for miracles. If there is no necessary conflict Hume needs to explain on what grounds one dismisses the positive evidence for miracles.

John: Even if you are right that still leaves open the possibility that the testimony in question is in fact unreliable.

Mary: I agree, but you cannot simply assume in advance of examining such testimony that it is unreliable.

John: I think you will find that when you do examine the evidence it is pretty poor. That is demonstrated very clearly by Hume's arguments in part 2.

Susan: Given that our time is running short, this is a good point at which to end. Next meeting, we will look at Hume's arguments in part 2. Now I invite you to partake of our customary wine and cheese.

4

HUME'S A POSTERIORI ARGUMENTS

Susan: Welcome to our fourth meeting of the Socrates Club. Today we continue discussing Hume's "Of Miracles," but move to considering the arguments found in part 2.

Holly: The four arguments of part 2 seem very different than the argument in part 1.

John: They are different. In part 1, Hume argues that we can always dismiss reports of miracles, since there must always be more evidence against a miracle than for it. In part 2, he claims that, even if you don't accept the argument in part 1, the actual evidence for miracles is extraordinarily poor.

Holly: So in part 1 he tells us we do not really have to look at reports of miracles to know that belief cannot be justified, but in part 2 he tells us that when we do in fact look, the evidence for miracles does not even come close to being convincing?

John: Yes, the argument in part 1 is a priori in the sense that he wants to claim there is no need to examine the testimonial evidence for miracles, since the evidence for the laws of nature with which it conflicts must always be greater and we must in the case of such a conflict always believe that for which there is the greater amount of evidence. The arguments in part 2 are a posteriori in the sense that Hume wants to claim that when one actually does look at the evidence for miracles it is of remarkably poor quality and should not be taken seriously.

Holly: I think I know what you mean by *a priori* and *a posteriori*, but just to make sure can you explain those terms. Not all of us are philosophy students, as I keep reminding you.

Prof. Roberts: These terms are from Latin. *A priori* means that the truth of a claim can be made independently of looking at particular cases, for example one does not have to check out individual bachelors to know that bachelors cannot be married. *A posteriori* means that the truth of a claim cannot be made independently of looking at particular cases, for example one must be prepared to check out all mammals before making the claim that no mammals can fly, otherwise one is going to be embarrassed to find that bats are in fact mammals that can fly.

Susan: What do people think of Hume's first a posteriori argument?

Brendan: You mean the one that goes,

> There is not to be found, in all history, any miracle attested by a sufficient number of men, of such unquestioned good-sense, education, and learning, as to secure us against all delusion in themselves; of such undoubted integrity, as to place them beyond all suspicion of any design to deceive others; of such credit and reputation in the eyes of mankind, as to have a great deal to lose in case of their being detected in any falsehood; and at the same time, attesting facts performed in such a public manner and in so celebrated a part of the world, as to render the detection unavoidable: All which circumstances are requisite to give us a full assurance in the testimony of men.[1]

Susan: Yes, that's the one.

1. Hume, *An Enquiry Concerning Human Understanding*, 150.

Mary: It seems more like an assertion than an argument. Just claiming something is the case is not an argument.

John: It is pretty obvious that a lot of miracle reports do not stand up to scrutiny.

Mary: That may be true, but it hardly justifies simply making a blanket assertion that none do. The fact that some miracle reports do not stand up to critical scrutiny does not demonstrate that there are not others that are well evidenced. It is not fair to pick out the craziest examples you can find and then conclude all reports fall into that category.

Holly: Would that be committing what you philosophers call the "straw man" fallacy?

Mary: Yes, tilting at a straw dummy is a whole lot easier that engaging with a real opponent.

Susan: I was thinking Hume might be guilty of a different fallacy—namely, begging the question.

John: Take it easy with all this talk of fallacies. All I said was that it seems pretty obvious that a lot of miracle reports do not stand up to scrutiny. That does not mean that I am guilty of setting up a straw man or begging the question.

Mary: Maybe not, but you seem headed in that direction. Why assume that because some reports are suspect that all are suspect? Why not take the reports on a case-by-case basis?

Brendan: That sounds good in theory, but if after we examine a lot or reports we never come up with ones that stand scrutiny, you can hardly blame John for thinking it is unlikely there are in fact credible reports.

Mary: It is not clear to me that John has done that. Has he systemically investigated a representative sample of miracle reports or has he just looked at the reports most easy to dismiss? Has he personally examined any reports or is he simply taking for granted that Hume and other skeptics are correct?

Susan: Let us leave aside those questions for the moment and stick to the text. What I want to know is whether Hume undermines his claim in this first argument that there are no credible reports of miracles, when he later discusses the Jansenist miracles?

Brendan: I am glad you brought that up. I wanted to explore that issue also. It seemed strange the way he raised a counterexample and then just dismissed it.

Holly (interrupting): Who were the Jansenists?

Prof. Roberts: The Jansenists were a group of Roman Catholics that followed the teaching of the theologian Cornelius Otto Jansen. They were opposed by another group within the Roman Catholic Church known as the Jesuits. A large number of miracles were reported to have occurred at the Jansensist convent of Port-Royal. One of the most famous of these miracles was the reported healing of the niece of the French scientist Pascal of a very serious eye ailment. This was so celebrated a case that the French king and queen sent their personal physician to verify the girl's healing.

Susan: What puzzles me and makes me wonder whether Hume was consistent is that when he discusses the Jansenist miracles he writes,

> Many of the miracles were immediately proved upon the spot, before judges of unquestioned integrity, attested by witnesses of credit and distinction, in a learned age, and on the most eminent theatre that is now in the world. Nor is this all: a relation of them was published and dispersed everywhere; nor were the *Jesuits*, though a learned body, supported by the civil magistrate, and determined enemies to those opinions, in whose favour the miracles were said to have been wrought, ever able distinctly to refute or detect them. Where shall we find such a number of circumstances, agreeing to the corroboration of one fact?[2]

Brendan: Yes, that passage and what follows is puzzling. One would expect him, after saying what you just quoted, to go on and

2. Ibid., 157.

argue that, appearances to the contrary, the requirements he set out in the first "argument" of part 2 were not really met in the case of the Jansenist miracles. He does not do that, however. Instead, he asserts,

> What have we to oppose to such a cloud of witnesses, but the absolute impossibility or miraculous nature of the events, which they relate? And this surely, in the eyes of all reasonable people, will alone be regarded as a sufficient refutation.[3]

I find it hard to see his response as anything but a retreat to the argument of part 1.

John: But if what he says about the Jansenist miracles is a retreat to the argument of part 1, why does he claim a little later that it would be possible to establish a miracle, just not a miracle as a foundation of a religion. The example he gives is:

> Suppose all authors, in all languages, agree, that, from the first of January 1600, there was a total darkness over the whole earth for eight days: suppose that the tradition of this extraordinary event is still strong and lively among the people: that all travellers, who return from foreign countries, bring us accounts of the same tradition, without the least variation or contradiction; it is evident, that our present philosophers, instead of doubting the fact, ought to receive it as certain, and ought to search for the causes whence it might be derived. The decay, corruption, and dissolution of nature, is an event rendered probable by so many analogies, that any phenomenon, which seems to have a tendency towards that catastrophe, comes within the reach of human testimony.[4]

Susan: It is interesting, however, that he immediately follows the example John cites with another example that seems equally compelling, yet he refuses to accept that the miracle could be accepted. He writes,

3. Ibid.
4. Ibid.

> But suppose, that all the historians who treat of England, should agree, that, on the first of January 1600, Queen Elizabeth died; that both before and after her death she was seen by her physicians and the whole court, as is usual with persons of her rank; that her successor was acknowledged and proclaimed by the parliament; and that, after being interred a month, she again appeared, resumed the throne, and governed England for three years: I must confess that I should be surprised at the concurrence of so many odd circumstances, but should not have the least inclination to believe so miraculous an event.[5]

Holly: Why does he treat those two cases differently and what is the relationship of these hypothetical examples to what he says about the Jansenist miracles.

Mary: I think the difference is that he treats the eight days of darkness example not as a genuine miracle, but as a marvel, that is to way as an event with natural, but unknown causes.

Holly: What makes you think that?

Mary: He says we ought to search for "the causes whence it might be derived." He would not say that if he thought it was an event supernaturally caused by God. Also, he says that it would be an event analogous to other natural events, thus suggesting it should be viewed as having a natural cause.

Holly: And in the case of the Queen Elizabeth example?

Mary: He treats that as a genuine miracle; that is to say as a violation of the laws of nature, and refuses to say that any amount of evidence could establish its occurrence.

Brendan: So we are back to Hume making a big deal of the marvel/miracle distinction?

Mary: Yes, and the point I want to stress is that he never really answers his own counterexample to what he claims in the first argument of part 2. Instead, he retreats to the argument he made

5. Ibid., 163–64.

in part 1 that we do not need to examine the evidence to reject reports of miracles. Rather than give reasons why the reports of the Jansenist miracles are not a legitimate counterexample to what he claims in this first argument, he goes back to insisting that all reports of miracles can be rejected on a priori grounds.

Brendan: Those grounds being that miracles must be defined as violations of the laws of nature, and that the evidence for the laws of nature will inevitably be greater than the evidence for miracles.

Holly: We have seen, however, that miracles need not be defined as violations of the laws of nature. So there is no necessary conflict between the evidence that establishes the laws of nature and the evidence in favor of miracles. That means that Hume is left without a good response to his own counterexample.

Mary: If there is a good response it cannot be on a priori grounds. If one wants to claim that there are no credible reports of miracles then one must actually examine cases such as the Jansensist accounts. That is what I meant earlier when I said that we have to proceed on a case by case basis. It will not do to assume that because some reports of miracles are not strongly evidenced, that none are.

Brendan: What about the second argument of part 2, where Hume claims that when

> the spirit of religion joins itself to the love of wonder, there is an end of common sense, and human testimony in these circumstances loses all pretension to authority. A religionist may be an enthusiast and imagine he sees what has not reality, he may know his narrative to be false and yet persevere in it with the best intentions in the world for the sake of promoting so holy a cause.[6]

Mary: I have the same problem with it that I had with the previous argument. It is an assertion rather than an argument.

---

6. Ibid., 151.

John: So you would not want to admit that common sense can be undermined when "the spirit of religion joins itself to a love of wonder"?

Mary: Saying something sometimes happens and saying it always happens are two very different claims. What evidence does Hume give for thinking that religious believers reporting firsthand experience of miracles invariably suffer from a deficiency of common sense or an undue credulity and love of wonder?

Brendan: Once again the Jansenist miracles come to mind. How is Hume going to deal with his own counterexample?

Susan: A feature of that counterexample that strikes me is that Hume says that the Jesuits, who were "determined enemies" of the Jansenists could not deny that the miracles happened. In the case of the Jesuits, their religious beliefs would have made them more, not less resistant, to the doctrinal claims made by the Jansenists. Yet Hume claims that the best they could say was that the miracles did not need to be taken as confirming Jansenist doctrine.

Holly: At the risk of sounding obtuse, what is your point?

Susan: That Hume is wrong to claim that religious belief will automatically predispose one to accept miracle claims. The Jesuits were not at all predisposed to accept Jansenist miracle claims. They were predisposed to reject them but, according to Hume, found the evidence too strong.

John: Perhaps you are being too hard on Hume. What he actually said was, "If the spirit of religion joins itself to the love of wonder, there is an end of common sense, and human testimony in these circumstances loses all pretension to authority."

Susan: My point is that you cannot assume that all religious people who believe in miracles do so because of "a love of wonder" which undermines their common sense. Some religious believers who accept that miracles occur are extremely rigorous in their examination of the evidence.

Prof. Roberts: John, if you doubt Susan's claim then you might want to examine what it takes for an event to be recognized as a miracle at Lourdes. There was a case at Lourdes where a man with a broken leg in which the bone was sticking through the skin, that is to say, a compound fracture, was instantaneously healed. The event was not officially recognized by the Catholic Church as a miracle, because there was no doctor in attendance to verify that it was indeed a compound fracture.[7]

Brendan: I think I would be prepared to consider it a miracle even if there was not a doctor present to pronounce officially that the man healed did indeed have a compound fracture.

Prof. Roberts: Yes, one of the people writing about the event made this point pretty vividly when he wrote that one does not have to be a tailor to recognize holes in a suit. It does, however, illustrate Susan's point that not all religious believers have succumbed to a love of wonder when they claim there is good evidence that a miracle has occurred.[8]

Holly: So on to the third argument.

Mary: I am not impressed with the third argument.

John: That is hardly a surprise.

Mary: That sounds suspiciously ad hominem.

Holly: I have to keep reminding you people that not everyone is a philosophy major. What do you mean by ad hominem.

Prof. Roberts: In Latin, the term *ad hominem* means "against the man," man being understood as the generic term for person. What is known as the ad hominem fallacy occurs when one attacks the person, rather than the person's argument. If John was suggesting that he could dismiss Mary's view of Hume's third argument simply on the basis that she is a Christian then he would be guilty of the ad hominem fallacy. The fact that Mary is a Christian cannot

---

7. Jaki, *Miracles and Physics*, 94–95.
8. Ibid.

be taken as ruling out the possibility she can give good arguments in support of what she claims.

John: I am happy to listen to Mary's reasons for saying that she is not impressed. I was just observing that I am not surprised that she does not like the argument.

Brendan: Susan, can you refresh our memory as to what the third argument is.

Susan: Hume says that

> it forms a strong presumption against all supernatural and miraculous relations, that they are observed chiefly to abound among ignorant and barbarous nations; or if civilized people has ever given admission to any of them, that people will be found to have received them from ignorant and barbarous ancestors, who transmitted them with that inviolable sanction and authority, which always attend received opinions . . . it is strange, . . . that such prodigious events never happen in our days. But it is nothing strange that men should lie in all ages.[9]

John: As I said earlier, I think the arguments of part 2 are not intended to function as Hume's chief reason for dismissing belief in miracles as inevitably irrational. I do not see, however, why Mary thinks this third argument is so bad.

Brendan: I hate to sound like a broken record, but what about Hume's own example of the Jansenist miracles. How can he say what he says in this third argument and then a little later admit reports of miracles contemporary to his own time that were in his words "immediately proved upon the spot, before judges of unquestioned integrity, attested by witnesses of credit and distinction, in a learned age, and on the most eminent theatre that is now in the world."[10]

John: Well he did say "observed chiefly to abound" did he not?

9. Hume, *Enquiry Concerning Human Understanding*, 152.
10. Ibid., 157.

Brendan: Yes, and then he says that any reports accepted by civilized people "will be found to have received them from ignorant and barbarous ancestors." How can such remarks be consistent with his example of the Jansenist miracles?

John: Ok, you have a point.

Mary: I agree that Brendan makes a good point. I think it is also important to ask what Hume means by "ignorant and barbarous." I have the suspicion that he would define as "ignorant and barbarous" anyone who believes in a miracle. That would make his claim true by definition which seems wrong.

John: I agree that Hume cannot make the claim that only ignorant and barbarous people believe in miracles true by definition. That would beg the question. It does seem correct, however, to think that people who lived long before the rise of science were insufficiently acquainted with the course of nature to distinguish a miracle from a natural event, so it is hardly surprising that most miracle stories come from before the rise of science.

Holly: Is the claim that most miracle stories come from before the rise of science really true? It seems that there are lots of contemporary miracle reports and Hume himself gives us the example of the Jansenist miracles in his times.

Susan: I agree that John would have to back up such a claim with empirical evidence, so it is a fair question to ask on what basis he makes it.

John: Perhaps I was a bit hasty in making that claim. It is my assumption, but I have to admit I have not researched the matter.

Mary: I think that John will be surprised if he investigates. I would be happy to point him to material dealing with contemporary accounts. I want to make a different point, however. The assumption that before the rise of science, people were incapable of recognizing a miracle as distinct from natural events is questionable. When Joseph found that Mary was pregnant, he was inclined to break the engagement.[11] He knew just as well as we do that virgins do not conceive in the normal course of nature. Likewise, one does not have to have a detailed knowledge of modern physics to realize that the multiplication of loaves of fishes does not occur in the normal course of nature.[12]

John: Mary, what about your earlier example concerning meteorites? An uneducated peasant of Laplace's time who saw a stone fall out of the sky might regard it as a miracle when it really has a natural explanation.

Mary: I am not so sure the peasant would regard it as miracle. Even if he or she mistakenly viewed it as a miracle it is nevertheless true that an uneducated person can be just as reliable an observer of a stone falling out of the sky as an educated person.

John: What is your point? It is pretty clear that meteors have a natural explanation.

Mary: My point is that the question of whether a certain event occurred or not, is distinct from the question of what its explanation is. Hume takes for granted that certain events, if they occurred, would be correctly described as miracles, but denies that we should ever believe such events have in fact occurred. The issue of how well educated someone is, seems to be more relevant to the question of what the explanation of the event is than to the question of whether the event occurred or not. An English student studying Dante can be just as good an observer of a stone falling out of the sky as a graduate student in astronomy.

John: So now you want to separate the question of whether an event occurred from the question of whether it is properly considered a miracle?

Mary: Yes. An event that is the result of as yet unknown natural causes is not a miracle.

11. Matt 1:18–20.

12. Mark 8:1–9.

John: How does that fit with what you said a few minutes ago, when you claimed that uneducated people could recognize a miracle. On your view, should they not just have recognized that the event occurred and remained agnostic about whether it should be called a miracle?

Prof. Roberts: John raises an important question and it is one that your discussion will have to deal with at some point, but you are straying a little from Hume. It is clear that he wants to deny that we have good reason to believe that reported events such as Jesus walking on water or multiplying food actually occurred, not that they would not be miracles if did occur. He takes for granted that if certain events occurred they would properly be deemed miracles.

Mary: If his grounds for making that claim are that uneducated people cannot be accurate observers then it seems a pretty weak argument.

Brendan: It seems that the problem with these three arguments is that they assert factual claims that need a lot more defense than Hume gives.

Mary: I think that you are going too easy on Hume. It is not that his factual claims need more defense, but rather that they are clearly false. Even if we were to accept the questionable claim that uneducated people cannot be trusted to give reliable testimony, it is true that reports of miracles do not only come from uneducated people, or from people with no common sense, or from people who lived before the rise of science.

Susan: If you people are finished beating up on Hume's first three arguments of part 2 what about the fourth argument? It seems different than the other three.

Holly: How so?

Susan: The first three depend on claims that are, to put it as charitably as I can, extremely dubious. The fourth argument looks a lot more like the argument of part 1, since it depends on a conflict of evidence.

Holly: And the conflict of evidence you are talking about is what?

John: A miracle which is evidence for one religion must be evidence against a rival religion. Since all religions claim miracles, the various miracle reports must cancel each other out. Hume puts it this way:

> Every miracle ... pretended to have been wrought in any of these religions . . . as its direct scope is to establish the particular system to which it is attributed; so has it the same force . . . to overthrow every other system. In destroying a rival system, it likewise destroys the credit of those miracles, on which that system was established; so that all the prodigies of different religions are to be regarded as contrary facts, and the evidences of these prodigies, whether weak or strong, as opposite to each other.[13]

Holly: You are right. This argument does seem a lot more like the argument of part 1, than the other three.

Susan: It seems an elegant argument, but is not Hume assuming that all miracle reports are on the same evidential footing?

Brendan: What are you getting at?

Susan: Hume takes for granted that the evidence supporting belief in the miracles of one religion can be no greater than the evidence supporting belief in the miracles of a different religion. Why assume that is the case in advance of actually examining the evidence? If it were to turn out that the evidence for miracles in a certain religion is very strong and the evidence for miracles in other religions is very weak, there exists no reason for seriously questioning the strongly evidenced claims and rejecting the weakly evidenced claims.

John: There would still be a conflict of evidence that would diminish the force of each miracle claim.

---

13. Hume, *Enquiry Concerning Human Understanding*, 154.

Susan: If one claim is much more strongly evidenced than another, I am not convinced there is a problem.

Holly: Why not?

Susan: Suppose in one tradition miracles are only ascribed to the founder of the religion centuries after that founder lived and in another tradition the miracles are ascribed by eye-witnesses during or shortly after the founder of that religion lived. Why I should take the weakly evidenced miracles as diminishing or cancelling the strongly evidenced reports? I think Hume oversimplifies the process of weighing evidence.

Mary: Also, it seems that miracles fit better in some religions than others.

Brendan: You are going to have to explain further.

Mary: If the religion in question has no room for miracles in its belief structure or if the founder of a religion or the early history of a religion rejected the idea of miracle then I would be more suspicious of miracle reports coming from that religion than I would of miracle reports coming from a religion in which miracles might be expected.

Brendan: How about an example?

Mary: Think about original Buddhism. Siddhartha Gautama taught that impermanence characterizes everything we see and was not committed to the existence of any kind of divine being. He discouraged his disciples from any interest in supernatural power on the grounds that enlightenment requires liberation from all desires. Miracles do not seem to fit with Buddhism in its early forms. The same could be said of certain forms of Hinduism that conceive of God as impersonal. If God is impersonal, that is to say as not having intentions or purposes, and a miracle is thought to be an act that furthers God's purposes, then adherents of those forms of Hinduism should not believe that miracles occur. Reports of miracles coming from such religions have less credibility than one's coming from theistic religions which view God as both creator and personal.

Susan: What if God did perform a miracle in such a religion?

John: Why would he?

Mary: Maybe to persuade them that he exists, is personal, and does have purposes. I think there is an even bigger problem with the argument than Susan has mentioned, however. I do not buy Hume's assumption that the chief purpose of a miracle is always to guarantee the truth of the religion in which it occurs. For example, I am a Christian, but I do not think that requires me to believe that God is not active in other religions.

Holly: So are you saying that all religions are equally good paths to God?

Mary: No, but neither am I saying there is no truth in religions other than Christianity.

John: But you, as a Christian, think Christianity contains more truth and is the superior, indeed in some sense the only way, to fully know God?

Mary: Yes, otherwise I would not be a Christian. I take very seriously Jesus' claim that he is the way, the truth, and the life and that no one can come to know God as Father except through him.[14]

John: So, as someone who believes that Christianity is the religion that contains the most truth why do you think God might do a miracle in a religion other than Christianity?

Mary: I think it is a mistake to see the sole or even chief purpose of a miracle to be that of guaranteeing the truth of a particular doctrine. I am drawing on my own tradition, but when Jesus is reported to have multiplied the loaves and fishes, he seems to have done so because people in the crowd were going to faint from hunger.[15] The miracle seems more a response to human suffering than an attempt to guarantee a theological doctrine.

John: It is an attractive thought to think that God is active in other religions and is willing to respond to human suffering

14. John 14:6.
15. Mark 8:1–9.

regardless of one's religion, but I think that you are going to have to grant one of Hume's main points if you say this.

Mary: And that point is?

John: Namely, Hume's claim "that no human testimony can have such force as to prove a miracle and make it a just foundation for any . . . system of religion."[16]

Mary: That is really two claims. First, I do not concede that human testimony is incapable of justifying belief in a miracle. Second, I do think that generally it is a mistake to see the chief purpose of a miracle to be that of guaranteeing the truth of a particular doctrine or religion. So I do not automatically take a miracle to be evidence of the truth of the tradition or religion in which it occurs. That does not mean it could never be the chief purpose of a miracle to validate a theological claim. Jesus seems to have claimed that the resurrection would count as validation of his claim to be the Messiah.[17] What I am claiming is that Hume cannot assume that reports of miracles in rival religions necessarily generate a conflict of evidence. God may have different purposes in performing different miracles, so that the occurrence of miracles in more than one religion does not demonstrate in itself any necessary incoherence in supposing that certain miracles could serve as "a just foundation for a system of religion." Saying this is not incompatible with my claim that miracles are generally performed for a reason other than the guarantee of doctrine.

Susan: Our time today is up. Thank you all for a lively discussion and now turn your attention to the desserts that Holly was kind enough to bring for today's meeting.

---

16. Hume, *Enquiry Concerning Human Understanding*, 163.

17. Matt 16:4.

5

MIRACLES AND UNEXPLAINED NATURAL EVENTS

Susan: Welcome everyone to our fifth meeting. Who wants to open the discussion today?

John: I will. We have spent a lot of time on Hume and, although I admire his argument of part 1, I concede that it is not as decisive as I first thought.

Mary: That is quite an understatement. It is not even close to being decisive. In fact, in light of the fact that miracles should not be thought of as violations of the laws of nature, the argument is irrelevant. If miracles do not violate the laws of nature then Hume is not in a position to speak of a conflict of evidence and his "balance of probabilities" strategy cannot even get started.

John: I am not willing to go that far, but perhaps we can agree to disagree as regards Hume. I want to raise a different criticism regarding belief in miracles. I think Hume would approve of it, though he does not raise it in "Of Miracles."

Brendan: What do you have in mind?

John: My criticism has to do with a point that Mary raised in our last meeting—namely, that the question of whether an event occurred needs to be distinguished from the question of what was the cause of the event. Hume assumes that if certain events occurred they would be miracles. For example, he is prepared to say, "It is a miracle that a dead man should come to life."[1] His argument is not that it would be wrong to label such events as miracles, but rather that we can never have sufficient evidence to justify believing reports of such events.

Brendan: Yes, that is what Hume tries to show, but you have not yet made clear this new criticism you want to raise.

John: It is this. Hume assumes that if certain events occurred it would be correct to view them as miracles, but denies we can be justified in believing they occurred. I suggest that even if one becomes convinced certain very unusual events take place, they should never be labeled miracles.

Brendan: Why is that?

John: Labeling an event a miracle cuts short any attempt to provide a scientific explanation of why it occurred and imposes an arbitrary limit on scientific investigation. What would happen to science if every time an unusual event for which we presently have no explanation is labeled a miracle and thus something science should not even try to explain?

Mary: You are claiming that to call an event a miracle is never legitimate?

John: Yes. You can never be justified in believing an event has a supernatural cause, it might have a natural but yet undiscovered cause. Calling an event a miracle makes science impossible, since it assumes in advance of scientific investigation that the event cannot be explained.

Holly: So you are claiming all events can be totally explained by natural causes?

1. Hume, *Enquiry Concerning Human Understanding*, 148.

John: No. I am simply claiming that science must proceed on the assumption all events can be explained in terms of natural causes.

Holly: How is that different from claiming all events can be explained in terms of natural causes?

John: I am not claiming that all events do in fact have natural causes, only that science must adopt a methodology that assumes they do. One can be a methodological naturalist without being a metaphysical naturalist, though I personally think the two go together well.

Holly: As someone working in the sciences I have to be a methodological naturalist, even if I am not a metaphysical naturalist?

John: Yes, that is what I am claiming.

Holly: So you are claiming that science requires that under no circumstances should an unusual event ever be called a miracle? Sounds like methodological atheism to me.

John: You could call it that I guess.

Mary: You are not asserting that miracles cannot occur, only that we could never be justified in believing in their occurrence?

John: Yes, I thought I had made my position clear. I am not claiming that science requires metaphysical naturalism, only methodological naturalism. I am not claiming that miracles cannot take place, only that one can never be epistemologically justified in believing they do.

Holly: I realize that each discipline has its own technical terms, but as a non-philosophy major I want to know what you mean by the term "epistemology."

Prof. Roberts: Epistemology is that branch of philosophy which studies how we justify our claims to know something. John is claiming not that miracles are logically impossible, in the sense that we know that God does not exist and thus that miracles cannot possibly occur, but rather that in the case of any particular unusual event we could never justifiably claim that it is in fact a miracle.

Holly: I get it. What philosophers call metaphysics is about what reality is like, what they call epistemology is about how we justify our claims about what reality is like.

Prof. Roberts: Right. We will make a philosophy major of you yet, Holly.

Susan: John's objection sounds pretty Humean to me. Like Hume, you are proposing an epistemological argument which a priori rules out the possibility of belief in miracles?

John: I agree that, like Hume's argument in part 1 of "Of Miracles," it a priori rules out the possibility of belief in the occurrence of miracles, but it does so for a different reason. I am not claiming one cannot accept the occurrence an unusual event on the basis of testimony, but rather that one can never be justified in claiming it is a miracle.

Mary: John, am I right in thinking that methodological naturalism amounts to the claim that it is never legitimate, even in principle, to postulate a nonnatural cause for a physical event?

John: Yes, that is a fair characterization.

Mary: Such a methodology guarantees that if a miracle does occur it cannot ever be recognized as such.

Brendan: Slow down, why do you say that?

Mary: We have said that methodological naturalism commits one to the claim that it is never legitimate, even in principle, to explain a physical event in terms of a nonnatural cause. That means, faced with events such as the virgin birth, or the resurrection, or Jesus turning water into wine, we must assume such events have a purely natural cause. Even if an event does not have a purely natural cause, methodological naturalism commits us to claiming it does. It guarantees we will never be able to label any physical event as a miracle and even if miracles actually occur they will never be recognized.

John: Even if I grant your argument, it is better to fail to recognize miracles than to make science impossible.

Mary: Just to be clear, you are committed to saying that no matter what the event or the context in which it occurs, it is never legitimate to view an event as a miracle; that is to say as an event that was supernaturally caused?

John: Yes that is correct; science has to assume that for any event it investigates the event has a natural cause.

Susan: So your claim is that science is only possible if we think of the universe as causally closed?

John: Yes.

Susan: What about the big bang cosmology we mentioned earlier? Would not the beginning of the universe be a physical event that scientists recognize as having no natural explanation?

John: I am willing to accept that there is no natural explanation for the big bang, but that just proves my point. If science is to explain an event it must assume there is a natural explanation for the event.

Brendan: How you are using the word "scientific"? If by "scientific" you mean "has a natural explanation," then I agree that belief in miracles is unscientific. If by "scientific" you mean "is capable of being systematically investigated empirically" then I think belief in miracles can be scientific. To pick up on Susan's example of big bang cosmology, our best methods of empirical investigation suggest that the universe had a beginning for which there is no natural explanation, but no one accuses scientists who accept the big bang of being unscientific. I see no reason why one cannot be scientific, yet open to the possibility that not all events have a natural explanation.

Mary: My concern is that a methodology which prevents us from ever recognizing a genuine miracle is fundamentally flawed. Theists are often criticized for not allowing any amount of evidence to falsify their belief in God, yet you are proposing a methodology which does not allow the possibility, even in the case of a genuine miracle, of ever falsifying the claim that the event has a natural cause. Are you not begging the question of whether miracles actually happen?

John: No, my point is that science is made impossible if you once start calling certain events miracles.

Mary: Such a claim is question begging. You need to justify your assertion that science would be made impossible if we were to recognize certain physical events as miracles. You cannot just assume that science and belief in miracles are incompatible.

Prof. Roberts: If I can intervene, let me suggest that both John and Mary have legitimate concerns. John is concerned that the ability of scientists to investigate nature not be undermined; Mary is concerned that science not be understood as ruling out the possibility of ever believing an event to be a miracle.

Susan: Is there any way of reconciling those concerns?

John: I do not see how. Methodological naturalism is our only protection against arbitrarily labeling any event not yet understood a miracle.

Brendan: So your concern is that there is no principled way to distinguish unusual events best understood as having a natural but unknown cause from unusual events best understood as having a supernatural cause, that is to say, miracles.

John: Yes, exactly right. There are no criteria which enable us to determine whether an unusual event should be understood as a miracle or simply taken as an indication of our limited understanding of natural processes. We must adopt methodological naturalism if we do not wish to place arbitrary limits on science.

Mary: I do not think that the decision regarding whether an unusual event should be labeled a miracle or not has to be arbitrary. I do not regard every unusual event I come across as a miracle.

John: So what is required if you are going to call an unusual event a miracle?

Mary: First, I would require that the regularity of nature to which the event is an exception is strongly confirmed and is known to apply to the same type of physical circumstances in which the event happened. It is because I have lots of evidence of how nature works in the cases of conception or death, that I would view the virgin birth or resurrection of Jesus as miracles.

John: Is that all that is needed?

Mary: No, I think the event has to fit with our broad conception of God's character and purposes. If someone prays for me when I am very sick and, contrary to what would be expected in the natural course of events, I get better I might interpret this as a miracle, since healing seems consistent with God's character. If, however, while I am out for a walk one day, I spontaneously burst into flame I would not be inclined to think of that as a miracle, but rather as an unexplained natural event, since it seems very difficult to view my bursting into flame as the direct intention of God.

John: Anything else?

Mary: It is important to take context into account. Recognizing whether an event is consistent with God's purposes may depend on how it fits into a broader pattern of events. As a Christian, I understand the virgin birth and resurrection of Jesus as part of a broader pattern of events and it is at least partially their place in that pattern that persuades me they are miracles rather than poorly understood natural events.

Brendan: Mary, is it your contention is that one can do science without adopting the assumption that the physical universe is causally closed?

Mary: It is not easy to define science. It is probably too simplistic to think of science as the search for natural causes, but even on such a definition I do not see why such a search has to presuppose that all events do, in fact, have natural causes. It seems to me that a rigorous and systematic search for natural causes might lead us to the conclusion that certain events cannot be explained in terms of natural causes. I realize that opens up the question of how we decide which physical events have natural causes and which do not, but I think the criteria I just gave show that such decisions need not be arbitrary.

John: I concede that Mary's criteria demonstrate that the decision whether to call an event a miracle or an unexplained natural event need not be arbitrary. I do not think, however, that she has dealt with the fundamental difficulty.

Brendan: That fundamental difficulty is what?

John: Although the initial decision to call an event a miracle may not be arbitrary, once an event is labeled a miracle we rule out any future scientific explanation of it.

Mary: How does that follow?

John: To call an event a miracle is to claim that it cannot be explained in terms of the natural causes science searches for. That means a miracle is scientifically inexplicable and thus beyond the reach of scientific investigation. Calling something a miracle, therefore, short circuits the possibility of future scientific investigation showing there are natural causes of an event we may have mistakenly labeled a miracle.

Mary: I want to make two points. First, I think it is a mistake to equate scientific investigation with commitment to explanation in terms of natural causes. Scientific investigation is consistent with acknowledging the existence of events which are inexplicable in terms of natural causes. Our best science points to what cosmologists tell us is a scientifically inexplicable "big bang" which is responsible for the physical universe. A principled search for natural causes does not require that such causes exist, so claiming that an event is a miracle does not imply it cannot be scientifically investigated.

Second, calling an event a miracle does not rule out the possibility of a future natural explanation of it. If new evidence were to emerge which shows that the regularity of nature to which the event is an exception is not actually strongly established, then I would conclude that I was mistaken in thinking that one of the requirements for judging it to be a miracle had been met.

John: So you are willing to say that you might be mistaken in calling an event a miracle?

Mary: Yes. If future scientific investigation provides a good explanation in terms of natural causes of the events I call miracles then I will cease to regard them as miracles.

John: You may have countered the objection that calling an event a miracle automatically rules out the possibility of a future scientific explanation of it, but doesn't your counter come at too great a cost?

Mary: You will have to explain what you mean.

John: You admit you could be mistaken in calling an event a miracle and that admission allows you to hold that you have not precluded the possibility that advances in science might someday show that what you thought was a miracle really was not. If that is true then is it not always more rational to believe that what we presently call miracles will someday have an explanation in terms of natural causes?

Mary: I do not see how that follows. The fact that a claim could conceivably be mistaken does not mean that it is likely that it is mistaken. The claim that arsenic in large amounts is toxic for humans could conceivably be mistaken, but it is hardly likely to be mistaken. My admission that I could conceivably be mistaken in calling an event a miracle does not commit me to saying I was probably mistaken in labeling it a miracle.

John: You have to admit that, supposing the events you want to call miracles actually happened, it is probable they have natural explanations.

Susan (interjecting): I think you say that because you are a metaphysical naturalist. I agree that if God does not exist then miracles are maximally improbable. If, however, you are a theist like Mary, or, like me, just open to the possibility that God exists, on what grounds would you be able to say it is improbable that miracles occur?

John: Do not go all metaphysical on me. I was thinking of the success that science has had in explaining what were previously thought to be miracles.

Susan: What kind of examples do you have in mind?

John: Well diseases used to be thought to be caused by evil spirits.

Mary: That does not seem a very good example, since it did not meet the first requirement I gave for an event being a miracle— namely, that it is an exception to a strongly confirmed regularity.

John: Nevertheless, people did attribute disease to supernatural influences.

Mary: I never said an event could be judged a miracle on the basis of superstition. I will give you that science has had success in explaining what were thought to be miracles on purely superstitious grounds. I do not think it has had much success in explaining events which meet the criteria I gave for calling something a miracle.

Holly: So the fact that some events are incorrectly termed miracles on less than rational grounds does not mean that there are not good reasons to view certain other events as genuinely miraculous.

Mary: That is exactly my point.

John: You are still a long ways from demonstrating that such events actually occur.

Mary: Granted, but my point is that whether there are such events should be determined by examining the evidence and not some a priori assumption that it could never legitimate to call an event a miracle.

Susan: I think there is another problem with John's argument.

John: What would that be?

Susan: You claim that the advance of science has demonstrated that events previously viewed as miracles have purely natural causes. Mary has challenged you to give some examples where the events falsely viewed as miracles were not posited as miracles on the basis of superstition, but rather met the criteria she gave for calling an event a miracle. I think that is a fair request, but the question I want to ask is whether you are prepared to admit that the advance of science might serve not to disconfirm a miracle claim, but rather to establish it more strongly.

John: Why do you say that?

Susan: If the advance of scientific knowledge can make a miracle claim less probable, does not it follow that the advance of scientific knowledge can make a miracle claim more probable? If the more we know about nature as science progresses the more difficult it becomes to explain an event in terms of natural causes should that not count in favor of the claim that the event is a miracle?

John: How about some examples?

Susan: If we were to take the virgin birth and the resurrection of Jesus as actually occurring has not the advance of science made it harder to explain these events in terms of natural causes rather than easier?

John: I am inclined to say those events did not take place so there is no need to explain them.

Mary: You are ducking the question. We have already established that the question of whether an event took place is distinct from the question of how it is to be explained. You began the discussion by granting the occurrence of the events in question but insisted it was a mistake to view them as having a supernatural explanation.

Brendan: I agree. It will not do to rule out the occurrence of certain events simply on the basis that if they occurred you cannot explain them in terms of natural causes.

John: Assuming the virgin birth and the resurrection of Jesus did actually occur, and in my mind that is a pretty large assumption, I would agree we have no plausible explanation of those events in terms of natural causes.

Susan: Would you agree that our increased knowledge of conception and physiology has made these events harder, rather than easier, to explain by means of natural causes?

John: Yes, but assuming these events did in fact occur, I am confident that the advances of science will explain them in the future.

Mary: That is a very large promissory note you are signing. In explaining such events as miracles the theist seems in a better position to be respectful of science than the atheist.

John: Ok, I will bite. Why is that?

Mary: At present, you have no explanation of how such events can be explained in terms of natural causes. Your rejection of an explanation in terms of supernatural causes is not based on the existence of an alternative explanation in terms of natural causes, but on the hope that one will become available in the future. If you are to provide such an explanation it seems that you must be prepared to reject or revise the presumed laws of nature which led you to expect different results. That means you are in the position of questioning what on other grounds appear to be basic, well-evidenced accurate statements of the laws of nature. In other words, you have to be skeptical as regards the current state of scientific knowledge.

John: I agree that it would not be easy to provide a natural explanation of such events, but why would you think the theist is in a position to be more respectful of science.

Mary: The theist is able to say why we may accept the occurrence of such extraordinary events without abandoning the basic trustworthiness of our scientific knowledge of how nature works. As we have seen, the occurrence of a miracle implies no violation or suspension of the laws of nature. For the theist, what is at issue is not whether we are entitled to trust well-confirmed laws of nature, but whether nature has in specific instances been intervened upon by a transcendent agent.

John: Are you denying that scientific knowledge is open to revision and growth?

Mary: What kind of revision and growth is going to explain the virgin birth and resurrection, but leave untouched what seems to be reliable knowledge of how conception and death usually operate?

John: I do not know, but who can say what science may look like in the future?

Susan: There is that promissory note again. No matter what the event you are going to assert that sometime in the future it will be shown to have natural causes. Your naturalism, whether it be methodological or metaphysical, seems to amount ruling out supernatural causes by fiat.

Mary: There is a further difficulty for naturalistic explanation. Earlier, I mentioned that the context in which an event occurs is relevant to judging whether it is a miracle. In the case of the virgin birth, for example, one would have to explain not only how Mary conceives, but the vision she has which predicts that she will conceive, and Joseph's angelic reassurance that she has not been unfaithful to him. Those events are all separate but form a teleological pattern that is going to be very hard for a naturalist to account for. Simply providing an explanation of how it might be possible for a virgin to conceive is not going to do the job.

Holly: There goes my suggestion of parthenogenesis. It would not explain the teleological pattern Mary is talking about.

Susan: Now who is using technical language? What is parthenogenesis?

Holly: Parthenogenesis is a form of reproduction in which an ovum develops into a new individual without fertilization. It occurs in a lot of insects naturally, and can be artificially induced in mammals.

Susan: Has it ever been observed in humans?

Prof. Roberts: No, it has never been observed in humans. Even if it had been observed in humans it could not explain the virgin birth of Jesus.

Brendan: Leaving aside the question of the larger teleological pattern that Mary mentioned, why not?

Prof. Roberts: Even if parthenogenesis were to occur in humans it could only result in the birth of a female child, since the ovum only has female chromosomes.

Brendan: Yes, Jesus being male would rule out his virgin birth being the result of parthenogenesis.

Susan: A good discussion, but once again we are out of time. Refreshments are waiting.

6

Miracles as Evidence for God

Susan: Welcome to our sixth meeting of the Socrates Club. So far, our discussions have proven very interesting and I am sure that today will not be an exception. The floor is open.

Brendan: Am I right in thinking that we concluded that if certain events occurred it would be more rational to view them as miracles than as events with unknown natural causes?

Susan: That certainly was not John's initial view; I am wondering if he has been convinced otherwise.

John: Yes and no. I have been partially convinced otherwise. It might under certain conditions be rational to view an event as a miracle, always assuming that it actually occurred, but I think Hume is right in saying that a miracle could never serve as evidence for a religion.

Holly: You are going to have to explain what you mean.

John: If you already believe in God it perhaps makes some sense to think that miracles can occur. A miracle, however, could never function as evidence for God.

Holly: That seems strange. When you ask most people who do not believe what it would take to make them believe they generally say a miracle.

Mary: Why can't a miracle be evidence for God's existence.

John: What was our definition of a miracle?

Susan: We said that a miracle is a dramatic supernatural intervention in nature in accordance with God's purposes.

John: So if God doesn't exist there cannot be miracles?

Susan: Yes. Something cannot be in accordance with God's purposes if God does not exist.

John: That means that a miracle cannot be evidence for God's existence, since in calling an event a miracle you have already presupposed that God exists. You are arguing in a circle if you claim the event is a miracle because God exists and then claim God exists because it is a miracle. Earlier in our discussions you kept saying that I begged questions, but that would be begging the question big time.

Mary: We have said that the question of whether an event has occurred is different than the question of what caused it.

John: I agree.

Mary: So your claim is not that one cannot establish the occurrence of the event without a prior belief in God, but that one cannot call it a miracle without a prior belief in God.

John: Yes, but what is your point?

Mary: Once we make that distinction, I do not think that your charge of begging the question holds up. To say that an event we are prepared to call a miracle cannot be evidence for God is like saying that a corpse we are prepared to call a homicide victim cannot be evidence for a murderer.

John: Calling the corpse a homicide victim commits you to the existence of a murderer. Have you not just reinforced my point that you have to believe in God before you can call an event a miracle?

Mary: My point is that the corpse, if it meets certain conditions, can be evidence of a murderer. It is true that once we call the corpse a homicide victim we are committed to the existence of a murderer, but we do not have to believe in a murderer in advance of there being a corpse, in order to justify explaining the corpse as a homicide. Similarly, you do not need to have a prior belief in God to be justified in calling an event a miracle.

Brendan: Why not?

Mary: In the case of the corpse all that is required is that we be willing to entertain the possibility of a murderer. If after investigation the corpse is best explained on the hypothesis of murder then we are justified in calling the corpse a homicide victim. In the case of an unusual event, all that is required is that we be willing to entertain the possibility that God exists. If after investigation its occurrence is best explained on the hypothesis that God exists then we are justified in calling the event a miracle.

Brendan: Ok, I get it. Your point is that the event can count as evidence for God's existence, even if one had no prior belief in God, just as the corpse can count as evidence for a murderer, even in the absence of a prior belief in a murderer. The label "miracle" or "homicide victim" is an expression of our judgment regarding how the event is best explained. We are back to the point that we made earlier—namely, that we must distinguish the question of whether an unusual event actually occurred, from the question of how it should be explained if it did occur.

Mary: Right. The issue is not whether you have to believe in God in order to believe that the event occurred, but whether you have to believe in God if you are going to explain its occurrence. We saw in our last meeting that the decision whether to call an event a miracle need not be arbitrary, so it does not seem right to suggest that someone who views such events as evidence for God is arguing in a circle. Assuming there is good evidence that an unusual event has occurred, it is legitimate to draw upon the hypothesis of theism in attempting to explain it, even if one did not previously accept the truth of theism.

John: I withdraw the question begging charge, but I emphasize that nothing that has been said is evidence that such events actually do occur.

Mary: I agree. My point is that you cannot rule out the possibility of establishing that such events occur and that they provide evidence for the existence of God.

John: Even if such events occur, calling them miracles does not really explain them.

Susan: Why do you say that? Are we not offering an explanation of their occurrence when we claim they are events caused by God intervening in the usual course of nature.

John: Not really. An event is explained when it is shown to be in conformity with a law of nature.

Susan: I thought we reached the conclusion in one of our earlier meetings that the laws of nature do not, by themselves, explain any event, but rather must be applied to an initial set of conditions.

John: I admit that initial conditions must be taken into account. My point is that the events you want to call miracles follow no consistently repeatable patterns and thus cannot be explained by reference to laws working on an initial set of conditions. Such events, if they occur, must be seen as unexplained moments of chaos in an otherwise orderly universe, not as evidence for God.

Mary: I do not see why you say non-repeatable. Miracles will recur when certain relevant antecedent conditions recur—namely, God desiring to perform another miracle. We have already established in an earlier discussion that miracles would not violate the laws of nature, so there is no need to view such events as moments of chaos.

John: But where is the pattern in such events?

Mary: The pattern would be found in God's intentions regarding the situation in which the miracle occurs.

John: So now we are supposed to be able to read God's mind in order to discern some kind of pattern?

Mary: We would not have to know God's thoughts completely to conclude an event was a miracle. If the event seems consistent with God's character and his purposes broadly understood, then there is no need to insist it is a moment of chaos. We often attribute events to human agency even though we do not know the agent's purposes completely.

Brendan: To pick up on what Mary has been saying, it is not clear that all explanations must involve appeal to some sort of law. I am a history major and in historical studies we often explain events in terms of an agent's purpose, rather than seeing them as instances of a law of nature. For example, if I were to donate a kidney to a relative whose kidneys were failing my action would be explained in terms of my goal of saving someone's life, not in terms of some uniform regularity of nature. Similarly, Caesar's crossing of the Rubicon would be explained not in terms of the laws of nature, but in terms of his decision to become emperor.

Susan: This is very interesting, but I want to raise another question. What is the relation of "the argument from miracles" to the more standard arguments for God's existence?

Holly: What do you mean by the standard arguments for God's existence?

Prof. Roberts: Arguments for God's existence tend to fall within general categories. At the risk of oversimplifying, ontological arguments claim that God's existence is implied by the concept of God, cosmological arguments claim that the existence of the universe requires the existence of God, teleological arguments claim that certain patterns within the universe require the existence of God, and moral arguments claim that the existence of morality requires the existence of God.

Susan: I do not see how the argument from miracle connects to ontological arguments, but I can see links to the cosmological, teleological and moral arguments. If miracles involve the creation of matter or energy that connects them to cosmological arguments, if they produce certain unusual patterns within nature that connects them to teleological arguments, and if they involve furthering divine purposes that connects them to moral arguments.

Brendan: You may be right, but do you want to claim it equally falls into all three categories of argument?

Mary: I think the cosmological, teleological and moral arguments are interconnected, so I agree to some extent with Susan, but, like Brendan, I would be uneasy about saying it equally falls into all three categories of argument. I think the "argument from miracle" is most naturally described as a kind of teleological argument, that is to say, as an argument from design.

Holly: Explain please.

Mary: Simply put the teleological argument is basically this:

> Premise: Nature, both as a system and in its parts, exhibits order.
>
> Premise: This order is best explained as the result of purposeful agency.
>
> Conclusion: Therefore nature is the result of a designing agent.

Brendan: I understand your summary of the teleological argument, but you have not explained why you think the "argument from miracle" should be described as a version of it.

Mary: Two reasons. First, the occurrence of events that might plausibly be viewed as miracles constitutes a further type of order that needs to be taken into account in explaining the overall order manifested by nature. Second, the occurrence of such events throws into question the adequacy of alternative explanations of order frequently given by atheists.

Brendan: I follow your first point, but I am not sure I follow your second.

Mary: Although the teleological argument is much broader than focusing on miracles would suggest, the occurrence of miracles might force detractors of the more general forms of the argument to rethink their explanations of other forms of order found in nature. For example, the miracle of the multiplication of the loaves and fishes might be thought to have implications for the issue of whether there have been supernatural interventions in the origin and development of life.

John: Whoa! That seems a pretty big stretch. Why would you say that?

Mary: If God created fish directly on one occasion, how can you be sure there weren't other occasions where he directly intervened in the process of life's origin and development?

Brendan: I assume you are thinking of the New Testament miracle of the loaves and fishes, where Jesus is reported as feeding a crowd on a small boy's lunch of loaves and fish.[1]

Mary: Yes.

John: Even if we were to grant that the event actually occurred, I hope you remember that those were dead, not live, fish.

Mary: Don't nitpick. My point is that, if there have occurred supernatural interventions in the course of human history, this suggests the strong possibility of supernatural interventions in prehistory. It does not prove such interventions took place, but it provides good reason to look critically at some of the speculative arguments that claim we can completely explain the type of order displayed by living organisms without reference to intelligence or supernatural intervention.

John: I suppose that if I took the occurrence of miracles seriously I might have to grant your point, but I do not think miracles

---

1. Mark 8:1–9.

happen. The way you were just talking makes you sound like a creationist. You aren't one of those are you?

Mary: It all depends on what you mean by the term "creationist." If by "creationist" you are suggesting that I believe the earth is only about ten thousand years old and that no natural processes played a significant role in the development of life, then no. If by "creationist" you mean somebody who thinks that, however long it took, the origin and development of life cannot be explained wholly in terms of natural causes then yes I am a creationist, or at least sympathetic to that position.

John: Are you not just quibbling over the use of words?

Mary: No. Taking seriously the possibility of divine intervention in the origin and development of life does not commit me to treating the early chapters of Genesis as some kind of scientific text and insisting that the earth is only ten thousand years old.

John: I thought you took Christian Scripture pretty seriously. Can you just arbitrarily pick and choose what you want to believe?

Mary: I am not being arbitrary. The early chapters of Genesis have to be read in the light of well-established hermeneutical principles. I think that when this is done, the Bible does not commit us to young earth creationism or the view that natural processes did not play a significant role in the origin and development of life.

Holly: Another technical term. What do you mean by hermeneutical?

Prof. Roberts: Hermeneutics is the discipline that investigates the principles of interpreting the meaning of texts. To give a really simplistic example, nobody reading a newspaper article in which a person is described as "hurling lightning bolts at her audience" should take that as literally claiming that the person was in fact throwing electrical charges at people.

John: Fair enough, but I doubt that the young earth creationists are going to accept that their understanding of Genesis is mistaken and that Mary's is right.

Mary: True, but I am prepared to argue for how I read the early chapters of Genesis.

Susan: I am sure it would be interesting to hear what Mary would say, but perhaps we can agree to leave that discussion for another time. Regarding our present discussion, I am inclined to accept that the "argument from miracle" is a type of teleological argument, but it seems an unusual one. What is usually at issue in evaluating the teleological argument is not the premise that nature exhibits order, but rather the premise that the amount and types of order it exhibits are best explained as the result of a designing agent.

Brendan: So critics tend to focus on the second premise of the argument rather than the first?

Mary: Yes, that is why we have the debate over whether the order displayed by living organisms needs explanation in terms of intelligent design. Atheists will grant that living organisms display a certain type of order, but suggest that the theory of evolution explains how such order can arise through non-intelligent natural causes.

Susan: In the case of the "argument from miracle," however, the debate tends not to be over whether this type of order requires a supernatural agent as its explanation, but whether this type of order really exists. Very few people would suggest that events such as the virgin birth or resurrection can be explained on any hypothesis other than a supernatural agent intervening in the usual course of nature. Many people, however, doubt that such events occur and thus that there is anything that needs to be explained.

Holly: So the advantage or at least potential advantage of the "argument from miracle" is that it presents us with an order or pattern that is very difficult to explain without positing supernatural agency.

John: That advantage is going to be purely hypothetical, unless you can demonstrate the occurrence of such events. You cannot just assume that such events took place and then argue that they are evidence for God's existence.

Mary: I agree that whether or not such events took place is a matter for investigation. What I want to insist on, is that it not be an investigation that has already prejudged the issue of whether it is ever rational to believe that such events occurred and that they could legitimately be viewed as supernaturally caused. That is why I think methodological naturalism must be rejected, since it guarantees in advance of actually looking at the data that no event could ever be recognized as a miracle.

John: I repeat my claim that you cannot simply assume that such events occur. I am not convinced there is any evidence that miracles occur.

Mary: That is hardly surprising, given that you adopt methodological naturalism. If you make the claim that it is never permissible, even in principle, to postulate a nonnatural cause for an event, you guarantee that evidence of supernatural intervention in nature will not be recognized, even if it exists. As for evidence, there is a great deal of testimonial evidence that miracles occur.

John: I have never seen an event that I would be prepared to call miraculous and I doubt that the testimonial evidence you talk of is very strong.

Mary: Have you ever seriously examined the testimonial evidence or have you just dismissed it out of hand?

Susan: We are scarcely in a position to investigate the empirical evidence.

Mary: I agree that our time does not permit this, but I want to emphasize that there is a substantial body of evidence in favor of miracles that deserves serious consideration. I would be happy to lend John some books if he would be willing to seriously investigate the evidence.

Susan: I think we have seen that the argument from miracle is one form or aspect of the teleological argument. Is it fair to say that how strong a form of the teleological argument it is depends on how good the evidence is for events that can plausibly be viewed as miracles?

Prof. Roberts: That seems a fair conclusion, though I think it deserves mention that philosophers and theologians generally agree the teleological argument does not provide a full argument for theism.

Holly: Why is that?

Prof. Roberts: Strictly speaking, the teleological argument only necessitates belief in a designer, not creator, of the universe.

Holly: A little more explanation, please.

Prof. Roberts: In our experience it is usually the case that the originator of order, say a sculptor, imposes order on some preexisting material that he or she did not create. Critics of the teleological argument, such as Hume, make the point that, even at its most successful, the argument only gets us to a designer of nature, not a creator of nature.

Brendan: Wouldn't it be pretty hard to think that the designer is not also the creator.

Prof. Roberts: I agree, but remember that I said strictly speaking.

Holly: You make it sound as if events such as Jesus' multiplication of loaves and fishes or his resurrection would not constitute powerful evidence for God. I think for most people such events would be compelling evidence for the existence of God.

Brendan: I agree. If I became convinced that such events occurred I would find them pretty convincing. They would be evidence that we cannot explain all reality in purely natural terms. Once I became convinced of that I would be very open to the God hypothesis.

John: But the God hypothesis would have to explain all the data that naturalism explains so well.

Brendan: Yes, but what would persuade me is that the God hypothesis, that is to say, theism, would be able to explain all that data, plus other data, that is to say events best understood as miracles, that naturalism cannot explain. So the importance of miracles for me would be that they would be a body of evidence that resists explanation on the worldview of naturalism, but can be explained on the worldview of theism.

John: I hope you are not assuming that such events in fact occur.

Brendan: No, but Mary has me persuaded that we cannot simply assume that they do not and that there would be nothing unscientific about the occurrence of such events. I am open to the possibility of there being good evidence for such events. Prior to our discussions I was not.

Mary: I do not think miracles constitute the whole case for theism, but I think they are an important part of it. So I think that they can, at least partially, serve as the foundation of religion.

John: You seem to be sliding from the hypothetical claim that if events we could plausibly construe as miracles occur then they would be evidence for the existence of God to the claim that such events actually do occur and are evidence for God.

Mary: I believe that such events occur and are evidence for God, but I do not expect anyone to accept their occurrence without investigating the evidence for their occurrence. What I have been arguing in these meetings is that you cannot settle the question of whether belief in miracles is rational by some a priori argument. Philosophers can't sit in ivory towers and decree what reality must be like.

Susan: Are you claiming that our philosophical discussion is just a preliminary exercise?

Mary: In a sense, yes. It is a very important preliminary exercise, but in my view the question of whether miracles actually occur cannot be resolved in the absence of historical investigation.

What is important is to make sure that the investigation does not short circuit itself by buying into questionable assumptions.

Holly: Such as insisting that methodological naturalism is essential to the practice of science?

Mary: Not to flog a dead horse, but yes. It often seems that people reject accounts of miracles not on the basis of detailed investigation of historical evidence, but rather on the assumption that belief in miracles is philosophically indefensible. What we are doing in our discussions is important as a ground-clearing exercise, but it is no substitute for examination of the historical evidence.

John: That sounds very empirical, but historians have to employ the principle of analogy—namely, that what occurred in the past is analogous to what occurs in the present. Our experience is that nature is regular and that must be the criterion by which we assess the trustworthiness of reports of miracles.

Prof. Roberts: That sounds a lot like Ernst Troeltsch. He wrote a very famous paper "On Historical and Dogmatic Method in Theology," in which he argued that

> analogy with what happens before our eyes and comes to pass . . . is the key to [historical] criticism. Deception, dubious dealings, fabrication of myth, fraud and party spirit which we see before our eyes are the means by which we recognize the same kind of thing in the material which comes to us. Agreement with normal, ordinary, repeatedly attested modes of occurrence and conditions, as we know them, is the mark of probability for the occurrences which criticism can acknowledge as having really happened or leave aside.[2]

John: He said it better, but that is basically my point.

Holly: How is that any different than Hume and his claim that there are no contemporary reports of miracles?

---

2. Troeltsch, "On the Historical and Dogmatic Methods in Theology," 13.

John: Even if there are present day reports of miracles they should be rejected as unhistorical, since they are not analogous to our normal everyday experience.

Susan: We seem back to Hume and the argument proving too much. Presumably, even if I were to observe an extraordinary event I would have to think I was deluded, since it is not analogous to my ordinary experience.

John: I do not think that works. We have experiences where something changed in the causal background and an unexpected event occurred. So we do have an analogy to work with.

Susan: What about our first experience of an unusual event? Why should we accept it, since it is not analogous to our usual experience?

Mary: I think there is a more fundamental objection to Troeltsch's objection. It is that miracles are analogous in an important respect to our normal everyday experience.

Holly: You are going to have to explain that claim.

Mary: I think this is a point we covered earlier. It is part of our experience that human agents can act to produce in nature events that would not otherwise occur. That seems analogous to what we are calling a miracle—namely, the action of a divine agent to produce an event that nature would not otherwise produce. As we have seen, neither human agents nor a divine agent has to violate any law of nature in producing such events.

Brendan: I agree with Mary, but it is one thing to say we cannot a priori rule out belief in miracles, quite another to say what would constitute enough evidence to justify belief in a miracle.

Holly: Seeing one would do it for me.

John: What about stage magicians? You cannot always believe what you think you see.

Holly: I meant under normal conditions. If I saw Jesus walking on water I think I could check pretty easily whether it was a trick or not.

Susan: Seeing one would be enough, but it is clear that for most miracles we have to rely on testimony.

Brendan: In principle, testimony could be supplemented by physical traces. If I had witnessed Lazarus' corpse but not been present when he was raised by Jesus my belief in the event would be considerably strengthened if Lazarus was around for me to talk to.

Susan: I agree, but physical traces tend to disappear over time. It is pretty clear that most miracles must be believed in on the basis of testimony. Certainly, the central miracles of a faith like Christianity must be believed on the basis of testimony rather than physical traces.

Brendan: What about the Shroud of Turin? Many people think that it provides evidence for the resurrection.

Susan: Even if it turns out to be authentic and there is lots of controversy over its authenticity, it would be the exception. We don't have any of the water that turned into wine, or the loaves and fishes that were multiplied and Lazarus is long gone. There is also the problem that even if such traces continued to exist we would only be convinced that they were in fact physical traces of a miracle if we could believe testimony surrounding their history. Presumably the loaves and fishes would look and taste the same as any other loaves and fishes, we would only know they were physical evidence of a miracle if we could believe the testimony surrounding their origin. So, although I want to say that physical traces could supplement testimony, I do not think they could stand as convincing evidence all by themselves independent of testimony.

Brendan: We seem to agree that miracles must generally be believed to occur on the basis of testimonial evidence. That raises the question of how we evaluate testimony.

Mary: A lot can be said about evaluating testimony, but if a report of a miracle comes from someone who I generally consider honest and a reliable observer then I take it seriously. If more than one such person reports the event I take it even more seriously.

Susan: But that does not take into account that people make mistakes, even if they have no intent to deceive. There are all sorts of circumstances in which perception or memory can play tricks on one.

Mary: I agree, but that is true not only in accepting reports of unusual events, but in accepting reports of ordinary events. The difficulties inherent in accurately reporting extraordinary events are often equally inherent in reporting ordinary events. It is no more difficult to be accurate in observing that water turned into wine, than in reporting some more usual event such as milk turning color and tasting sweet and chocolate when you add cocoa and sugar. So if an author, say Luke in the New Testament, has proved reliable in reporting ordinary events of geography and history that should count as reason to think he is probably reliable in reporting unusual events such as walking on water or the multiplication of loaves and fishes.

Brendan: But surely it is going to be easier to trust reports of usual events than unusual events?

Mary: If you are assuming that it is easier to be accurate in observing ordinary events than extraordinary events, I disagree. It would be a lot easier to be correct about reporting one's seeing water turning into wine, than to be correct in reporting some obscure point of protocol. So if someone, say Luke, the writer of one of the Gospels, were to be accurate in his reporting of ordinary detail that is not easy to get right, I think it would count towards trusting his report of unusual events.

John: Did Luke claim to have personally witnessed all the miracles he reports.

Mary: No, but he does claim to have witnessed some of them. Also, he was in a position to assess whether the people who did report witnessing the events were credible.

John: I think it fair to point out the contrast between our scientific beliefs and belief in miracles. In science we believe things because we can repeat the experiment and get the same result. Science is based on direct observation of events, belief in miracles is based on testimony.

Mary: Testimony is a lot more central to science than you seem to be suggesting. The body of scientific knowledge is so big that no one scientist can experimentally test any but the smallest fraction of his scientific beliefs. Most of what any scientist believes is believed on the basis of what he or she considers trustworthy testimony.

John: Scientific claims can be tested. We can experiment and see if the same event takes place again.

Mary: It would not be the same event that takes place, but a similar one produced under similar circumstances. You may boil water twice, but it is two different events of boiling.

Holly: Are you not just splitting hairs, Mary?

Mary: No. I agree that the water boiling the second time, that is to say, acting in a similar manner to our first observation, gives us reason to trust our first observation. The same point, however, is true as regards testimony. We may observe that testimony given under certain similar sets of circumstances tends to be reliable and have that count towards our trusting a particular report given under those types of circumstances.

Holly: Can you put your point more generally?

Mary: Two points actually. First, scientists depend on testimony just as essentially as historians. Second, the evidence for testimony occurring under certain conditions being reliable can mount up in the same way the evidence for a law of nature can mount up.

Holly: So we are saying that in principle it is possible to establish on the basis of testimony the occurrence of events best understood as miracles, and that the actual occurrence of such events would constitute strong evidence for God?

Susan: That seems a fair summary of today's discussion.

John: So long as we are speaking hypothetically, I agree. I want to stress, however, that there is no good evidence for miracles.

Mary: Surely that remains to be determined. I think you ought to be open to looking at those books I offered to lend you.

Susan: I am sorry to say that once again we are out of time. We will meet next week at the same place and time.

7

MIRACLES AND THE PROBLEM OF EVIL

Susan: Welcome to our seventh and, for this term, final meeting. Who wants to start today?

Brendan: Something about the concept of a miracle bothers me. Miracles are defined as supernatural interventions in nature in line with God's purposes, but if God is perfect, that is to say, all powerful and all knowing, why would miracles be necessary.

Holly: What do you mean?

Brendan: Does it not seem that interventions would not be necessary if things were done right in the first place? Miracles make God seem like a bit of a bumbler.

John: I agree. Constantly having to tinker with creation seems inconsistent with the perfect God theists like to talk about.

Holly: You make creation sound like a machine.

John: What is wrong with that?

Mary: In the case of a machine it is tempting to say that the more perfectly it is designed, the less its creator needs to adjust it. So, the better a clock is, the less one has to worry about setting it. However, what if one thinks of creation, not along the lines of something like a clock, but something like a musical instrument, say a violin?

John: What are you getting at?

Mary: A clock and a musical instrument are equally products of design, but a clock is designed not to be interacted with whereas a violin is designed to be interacted with. You cannot assume that a creation in which God intervenes is less perfect than one in which God does not. It all depends upon what God's purposes are in creating the universe. Maybe God creates the universe intending to intervene at certain points in its ongoing development.

John: To say that God intervenes in the course of nature seems to suggest that he acts as one cause amongst many other causes in the world. I would think that theists would not want to reduce God to the status of one cause amongst many. Miracles seem to diminish God from almighty Creator to just one more causal agent acting in the universe.

Holly: Let me get clear what you are saying. You want to claim that the idea of the Creator of the universe performing miracles is theologically inadequate.

John: Yes, that is right. Even if one is a theist, one should not believe in miracles.

Holly: I don't see why. Surely if God is the creator of the universe he can act in it.

John: If God is seen not as the author of the universe and all the causes that operate in it, but simply as one of the causes operating in it, that reduces him to the status of simply being a part of the universe.

Mary: You seem to be claiming that either one must view God as creator of the universe, in which case he cannot intervene in its workings, and thus no miracles, or he can intervene in its workings, in which case he could not be the Creator of the universe.

That just seems wrong. If I create an aquarium there is no reason to think I could not intervene in its working and if I do intervene in its working that hardly reduces me to the status of a fish.

John: Do you really want to compare the universe to an aquarium?

Mary: It would be easy enough to pick a different analogy. My point is that there is no good reason to think that the creator of something might not intervene in its working. If she does so it does not make her part of the thing she made. Neither does it mean that she is a bumbler.

Holly: I am with Mary on this one. I do not see any contradiction between believing that God is the cause of the whole universe and believing that he sometimes intervenes in what happens in the universe. If directors can act in their own movies I do not see why God cannot intervene in his own universe.

John: Does that not prove my point? When Hitchcock took a part in his own movies he became part of the movie.

Mary: But in so doing he did not cease to be the director? Does that not prove my point?

John: What I want explained is how God can be both the cause of the universe, and thus the cause of everything that happens, and operate, in the case of intervening miraculous events, as one cause amongst many in the world.

Mary: God causes things to exist, but once they exist they have a nature of their own and interact causally with other created things. So we can speak of secondary causes, that is to say created things with causal powers. God can act indirectly through the effects of secondary causes or he can act directly upon created things. I do not see any contradiction or theological inadequacy in saying that God is both the cause of all that exists, yet can act as an agent in creation. The idea of God humbling himself and entering creation under creaturely conditions is at the heart of the Christian faith.

John: You cannot establish a philosophical point by appealing to your faith tradition.

Mary: I didn't. I explained why I hold that God can be the cause of all that exists, yet also act directly in the world. I mentioned Christianity in order to show that at least one of the major faith traditions believes that God can both be the cause of the universe, yet act directly within it.

Brendan: Is not the idea of free will also relevant? If humans have genuine freedom then it does not seem implausible to think that God might sometimes adapt his actions to human choices.

Holly: Would he not have to? If people are genuinely free they can presumably choose from a range of alternatives. If God wants to achieve certain goals and also respect human freedom it seems to make sense that he may adopt his actions in response to human choices.

Mary: There are examples in what we Christians call the Old Testament which seem to suggest that what God brings to pass depends on human choice.

Susan: How about giving us one?

Mary: I could come up with other examples, but one instance can be found in Jeremiah 26:2–3. In the New King James Version it reads, "Thus says the Lord: 'Stand in the courts of the Lord's house, and speak to all the cities of Judah, which come to worship in the Lord's house, all the words that I command you to speak to them. Do not diminish a word. Perhaps everyone will listen and turn from his evil way, that I may relent concerning the calamity which I purpose to bring on them because of the evil of their doings.'" If we take those verses at face value they seem to suggest that God is not only active in history, but that he alters his actions in response to human choices.

Brendan: I thought this was a philosophy club. Why should I take the Old Testament as a reliable source of information about God?

Susan: I do not think that is fair, Brendan. I asked Mary for an example. I agree the issue is not the authority of Christian Scripture, but whether it makes sense to think that God might intervene in creation in response to human choices. I do not think it is irrelevant, however, that in what purports to be a revelation from God we find instances where God is said to intervene on the basis of human choices.

John: I agree that we should not be misled by the metaphor or analogy we use to describe the universe. I also agree that if genuine human freedom exists it makes sense to think that certain of God's actions in history might be contingent on that freedom. I think a deeper problem is being missed, however.

Brendan: That problem would be what?

John: Miracles seem purely arbitrary. There appears no rhyme or reason in their occurrence.

Susan: How so? We have said that an event cannot be a miracle if it is not in accordance with what we take to be God's purposes.

John: An instance of, say healing, may be accordance with what we take to be God's purposes, but it is pretty clear that not everybody receives healing. How is that consistent with God being just? Why should one person get healed but not another?

Mary: You seem to be claiming both that it is unworthy of God to perform any miracles and that he should perform more miracles. How is that consistent?

John: Leaving aside our disagreement whether God should ever intervene in nature, I want to claim that if he does intervene in nature he ought to distribute miracles in a less arbitrary fashion.

Mary: So it is wrong for God ever to intervene in nature, but it is also wrong that he does not intervene more often?

John: I am willing to grant for the sake of our discussion that perhaps God performs miracles from time to time. What seems clear though is that there is no rhyme or reason to who gets a miracle. If God does perform miracles he is less than just, since some people get them and others do not.

Mary: I do not know why one person would get healed but not another, but it seems to me that a healing lessens the amount of evil in the world. Why would you think that an event that lessens the amount of evil in the world counts against the existence of God?

John: I do not deny that someone getting healed is a good thing and that, at least in one sense, it lessens the amount of evil in the world. In another sense, however, it increases the amount of evil in the world. How can we think of God as perfectly just if not all people in similar circumstances are treated in the same manner? Why should some people dying of cancer get healed while others do not?

Mary: Health is a good, but not as high a good as some other goods. Maybe sometimes suffering points us to important things in life we would not otherwise pursue or notice.

John: What you say might sometimes be true, but it does not cover all cases. Sometimes suffering, especially if it is too intense, tears down rather than builds up a person's character.

Mary: I do not think there is any easy answer to the problem you raise, but I think there are good reasons for thinking it is not as conclusive an objection as you suggest.

John: I wonder what those would be.

Mary: Well, at least in my faith tradition, miracles tend to involve cooperation between God and a human through whom God works the miracle. It seems possible that there are instances where God would be willing to perform a miracle, but the person through whom he wants to work the miracle may be unwilling or too afraid to cooperate. For example, when Ananias is told to go and pray for Saul that Saul may receive his sight, he is being asked by God to heal a man who has a reputation of killing and imprisoning Christians. It could not have been an easy thing for Ananias to do or even to trust that he had really heard from God.[1]

Holly: So maybe God would like to perform more miracles than actually occur, but the people whom he wants to work through are not prepared for the risks that involves.

Mary: That is what I am suggesting, though I do not want to claim that it constitutes anything like a complete answer to John.

Susan: Also, it seems clear that those who receive miracles do not necessarily have a more easy life than those who do not. In the passage Mary mentioned, in addition to being healed of blindness, Paul is told that he will suffer greatly. Writing later, Paul tells his readers that he was flogged five times, that he was beaten with rods three times, that he was shipwrecked three times and that hunger, sleeplessness, and threat of being robbed were routine conditions of his ministry.[2]

Mary: There is also the point that if God's intention is to build character he might achieve his goal through means other than miracles. In fact miracles might sometimes be a detriment to developing character.

Brendan: How so?

Mary: Well if God were always to save us from the consequences of bad choices by means of a miracle, would we care about the choices we make? If I could know that it did not matter whether I put my hand on a hot stove burner because God would protect me from harm by performing a miracle, why would I care where I put my hand?

John: Even if I grant you that these suggestions go some ways towards explaining why miracles occur in some instances but not in others, they do not provide anything close to a complete answer to my argument.

1. Acts 9:10–18. After his Damascus Road experience, Saul changes his name to Paul.

2. 2 Cor 11:24–27.

Prof. Roberts: Perhaps that is not surprising, since your question of why miracles occur in some instances but not in others seems essentially a form of the problem of evil.

Holly: I know I keep asking this, but explain further please.

Prof. Roberts: John's question raises the issue of why if God is prepared to eliminate some evils by performing miracles, why does he not eliminate more evil? I am not sure that we can ever completely explain why God allows evil.

John: It sounds as if you are admitting that belief in God is irrational? I did not think that was your position.

Prof. Roberts: It isn't.

John: But did you not just admit that theists cannot completely explain why God allows evil?

Prof. Roberts: Yes, I did. However, before I try and explain why what I said does not commit me to saying that belief in God is irrational, I want to stress that the issue is not whether God is justified in allowing some evils—clearly he is—but whether there exist evils God is not justified in allowing.

Holly: You are going to have to explain that last remark for me.

Prof. Roberts: It seems impossible to conceive of a physical environment which does not allow for what are called natural evils, that is to say evils which are not associated with moral choice.

Holly: Some examples of what you mean by natural evils would be helpful.

Prof. Roberts: I have in mind events such as getting wet if you are caught outside in a rainstorm, or hurt if you have a heavy branch fall on you when you are walking in the woods. Natural evils do not occur as a result of the misuse of free choice, but just seem inherent in the nature of the world.

Holly: You mentioned moral evils. What about those?

Prof. Roberts: If God creates a world in which genuine free will operates then people are capable of making bad choices that lead to evil.

Brendan: So why create a world with free will?

Mary: Because a world with free will is better than a world without free will, even if free will can lead to certain evils that would not otherwise occur.

John: I grant your point that the problem is not with God allowing evil, but rather with God allowing unjustified or pointless evil. I do not see how that resolves the problem. It seems pretty clear to me that there is unjustified evil in the world.

Prof. Roberts: My point is that there is no logical contradiction between the claim that God exists and that evil exists.

John: Do you grant that there is a contradiction between the claim that God exists and that unjustified or pointless evil exists?

Prof. Roberts: Yes. What I want to emphasize, however, is that evils do not come with labels attached telling us whether they are pointless or not. The claim that an evil is genuinely pointless must take into account all the evidence. If there is lots of evidence for God's existence then that is also good evidence that there are no genuinely pointless evils, even though we may not be able to say what the point is.

Brendan: I get it. You cannot simply consider the negative evidence, that is to say evils that we cannot see a point to, but also the positive evidence for God and that would include the occurrence of events plausibly viewed as miracles.

John: Always supposing that such events did in fact occur.

Susan: I think there is another point that needs to be made in defense of theism.

John: Ok, let us hear it.

Susan: Evil seems to be a problem for every worldview. Given that there is no logical contradiction between the existence of evil and the existence of God, and given that if there is good evidence for God then there is good evidence that there are no genuinely pointless evils, the existence of evil will only count as a reason to reject theism if there is some other worldview that provides a better solution to the problem of evil. So the question is not whether evil is a problem for the theist, but whether it is a bigger problem for the theist than for non-theists.

John: Evil is not a problem for materialists. What people call evil amounts simply to our subjective preferences running counter to natural process. My preference is not to get struck by lightning, but if through no fault of my own I am caught out on a lake in the middle of a thunder storm there is a pretty good chance it could happen.

Mary: I find it significant that you used the phrase "through no fault of my own." How are you going to explain moral evil, that is to say evil arising from free will?

John: Simple, I do not believe in free will. People are wholly a product of their heredity and environment. Free will is prescientific myth.

Brendan: That reminds me of the teenager that was getting lectured by her parents for a bad report card. After her parents had gone on at length, she looked at them and said, "I know it is a really terrible report card. Do you suppose heredity or environment is to blame?"

Holly: Funny joke, but what is your point? Are you just trying to lighten the mood?

Brendan: There is a serious point to my joke. Does John really want to claim that we should never hold people morally responsible for their actions? That seems to undermine some of our deepest intuitions. If that is a consequence of materialism, then I think that counts as a pretty big reason to reject materialism. If I went over to John and kicked him in the shins I am pretty sure he would blame me and not my shoe, but if what he is saying if correct, why should he hold me responsible? Ultimately, on his view, I am just as determined by prior events in the history of the universe as my shoe is.

Susan: If he is wholly a product of his environment and heredity then perhaps he cannot help holding you responsible, even if it is not rational to do so.

Brendan: If we say that, then we are saying that the assignment of moral responsibility is never rational. I do not think that many people, whatever they say, really believe such a claim.

Holly: What about pantheism? What if everything is part of God? Does not such a worldview eliminate any problem of evil?

Mary: I do not think it does. If everything is part of God then is not everything that happens equally an expression of God?

Holly: Yes, that makes sense, but what is your point?

Mary: Well if everything is equally an expression of God then Hitler and Saddam Hussein were equally an expression of God's nature as Mother Teresa and Gandhi.

Susan: I see what you are getting at. Pantheism leads to the same conclusion as John's materialism—namely, that what we call good and evil are only expressions of our subjective preferences.

Holly: The other day I heard someone using the term "panentheism" and she seemed to want to distinguish it from both theism and pantheism. What is panentheism and where does it fit into the picture? How does it deal with the problem of evil?

Prof. Roberts: Put very simply, panentheism is the view that the world is part of God, but not all of God.

Susan: I do not see how that gets us past pantheism's claim that good and evil are only expressions of our subjective preferences. If the world is part of God then presumably all parts of it are equally expressions of God's nature and there is no reason to think Hitler is any less an expression of God's nature than Mother Teresa.

Mary: Another point is that if panentheism is true then the universe must have always existed.

Holly: Why do you say that?

Mary: If God is eternal and the universe is part of God it seems the universe would have to be eternal. How can the universe be part of God if, as our best cosmology indicates, it had a beginning?

Holly: Would not what you are saying also apply to pantheism? How if God and the universe are identical can the universe have had a beginning, yet God be eternal?

Prof. Roberts: I think you have a point Holly, though some pantheists maintain that the universe, including ourselves, is an illusion and not really there.

Brendan: That seems a pretty hard claim to swallow. Especially since, if the universe does not exist and we do not really exist, you have to ask who is having the illusion.

Susan: Also, we think of illusions as something evil, so the pantheist has not really explained evil away if he calls evil an illusion.

Brendan: I did not initially find his claim persuasive, but I think Prof. Roberts is right when he claims that the problem of evil is a problem for all worldviews and not just theism. If evil is as big or bigger problem for other worldviews it cannot function as a reason to reject theism in favor of some other worldview.

Mary: For me, approaching philosophy from my faith tradition of Christianity, I find it significant that Jesus, who I believe to be God incarnate, entered into our human suffering and experienced a degree of suffering that most humans never have to go through. That reassures me that, whatever the reasons for God allowing suffering, he cares about what we go through.

Brendan: So you think that God suffers?

Mary: Yes. Both in the Old and New Testaments, God is said to grieve over human suffering. I do not think that is just mistaken anthropomorphic language and I do not think that when Jesus wept at Lazarus's grave that he was somehow grieved only because he was physically incarnate.

Brendan: Interesting. I wonder how that fits with other theological claims concerning the nature of God.

Susan: I am afraid we are going to have to end it here. As a celebration of the end of term Prof. Roberts has invited us all for dinner at his house. Wine will be served, but if we run out, he tells me he is in no position to turn water into wine.

Prof. Roberts: Before we head out for dinner, I want to mention that I have put together some actual reports of miracles. Two of these reports, the ones from Augustine and Pascal, can be found in books, but the others are ones I have collected from people I personally am acquainted with.[3] My purpose in giving you these is that in the course of these discussions we seem to have arrived at the conclusion that, although philosophers can talk about how miracles can be defined and what types and amounts of evidence would be relevant to deciding whether miracles occur, in the final analysis one will have to investigate actual accounts to determine whether miracles have in fact happened.

John: I am pretty skeptical that your reports will prove convincing.

Mary: I think you should have been named Thomas rather than John.

Brendan: I get it. Doubting Thomas.

John: Very funny.

Mary: Sorry John, I shouldn't tease. Let us go to dinner and agree to disagree.

John: Sounds good to me.

---

3. These are real and not fictional cases. See appendix.

Appendix
Six Healing Cases

CASE 1

AUGUSTINE, WRITING LATE IN the fourth century and early in the fifth, was the most influential theologian of the early Christian church. In his early writings, Augustine was prepared to say that miracles played an essential role in establishing Christianity, but that they had ceased to occur. In his work *Of True Religion*, he wrote:

> We have heard that our predecessors, at a stage in faith on the way from temporal things up to eternal things, followed visible miracles. They could do nothing else. And they did so in such a way that it should not be necessary for those who came after them. When the Catholic Church had been founded and diffused throughout the whole world, on the one hand miracles were not allowed to continue till our time, lest the mind should always seek visible things, and the human race should grow cold by becoming accustomed to things which when they were novelties kindled its faith. On the other hand we must not doubt that those are to be believed who proclaimed miracles which only a few had actually seen, and yet were able to persuade whole peoples to follow them. At that time the problem was to get people to believe

before anyone was fit to reason about divine and invisible things.[1]

Augustine later retracted his early view, coming to believe both on the basis of testimony and personal experience that

> the truth is that even today miracles are being wrought in the name of Christ . . . Such miracles do not strike the imagination with the same flashing brilliance as the earlier miracles . . . The fact that the canon of our Scripture is definitively closed brings it about that the original miracles are everywhere repeated and are fixed in peoples' memory, whereas contemporary miracles which happen here or there seldom become known even to the whole of the local population in and around the place where they occur.[2]

Augustine immediately follows this observation with an account of a miracle he witnessed personally. He writes,

> Only a handful of people have ever heard of a cure that occurred in Carthage when I was there and which I witnessed with my own eyes. It happened to Innocent, a former advocate in the office of deputy prefect, at the time when my fellow bishop, Alypius, and I (neither of us yet ordained, but both already dedicated to God) had just returned from Italy. Innocent, along with his whole household, was a remarkably devout Catholic and he welcomed us into his home. He was just then undergoing medical care in connection with a complicated case of multiple rectal fistula [anal abscesses]. The doctors had already incised and were now following up with applied medications. The cutting had caused very acute pains and these continued day after day, the trouble being that one of the sinuses that should have been opened was so recessed that it had escaped the scrutiny of the surgeons. Long after all the other sinuses were healed, this single one remained, and all efforts to relieve the patient's pain were unavailing.

1. Augustine, *Of True Religion*, 25.47.
2. Augustine, *City of God*, 22.8, 433–37.

Naturally, he became afraid that a second operation would be called for, particularly since his family doctor, who had not been allowed even to watch the original operation, had told Innocent that this would be the case. On that occasion, Innocent had become so annoyed that he dismissed the doctor from his service. His anxiety, however, continued. One day, in fact, he turned to his surgeons and burst out: "Do you mean to cut me again? Don't tell me that the man you refused to admit to the operation was right after all!" The surgeons, however, merely scoffed at the family doctor's naiveté and tried to calm their patient and, in their best bedside manner, made soothing promises.

But, as day after day dragged on, nothing came of all their medications. The surgeons kept saying that there was no need to operate and that all would respond to treatment. However, they called in for consultation Ammonius, a very old and famous practitioner, who has since died. He examined the patient's rectum and, on the basis of the other surgeons' technique and aftercare, gave the same prognosis as they. Innocent, for the moment, was so assured by the weight of this authority that he began to talk as though he were already cured. He even indulged in cheerful banter at the expense of the poor family doctor who had predicted that more cutting was to come.

Well, to make a long story short, so many days passed to no purpose that the worn-out and humbled surgeons confessed, at last, that nothing short of the scalpel would effect a cure. Poor Innocent turned pale with fear and nearly fainted. As soon as he was sufficiently calm to talk, he told them to get out and never come back again. Worn out with weeping and with no other recourse, he thought that the best thing he could do would be to call in an extremely skillful surgeon from Alexandria, and have him do what he was too angry to let the other surgeons do. This world-famous specialist came, and examined with his trained eye the excellent work the others had done, as was clear from the healthy residual scar tissue. Whereupon, the specialist behaved like a man of principle and persuaded Innocent to allow the surgeons to have the satisfaction of terminating a case on which they had obviously worked so well and so long. He admitted that no cure was possible without a second operation, but protested that it would be utterly against his professional ethics to deprive others of the satisfaction of completing an operation in which so little remained to be done and, especially, to deprive men whose skillful work and careful handling of the patient he so much admired. So the surgeons returned to the good graces of Innocent, and it was agreed that they should incise the remaining sinus in the presence of the Alexandrian specialist. The operation was set for the next day, all the doctors admitting that it was the only way to heal the trouble.

Once they were gone, the whole household set up a wail of grief for their master that was worse than a funeral, and we had the hardest time keeping them calm. Among Innocent's habitual visitors who happened to be there that day were that holy man of blessed memory, Saturninus, then Bishop of Uzalum, and Gulosus, a holy priest, and some deacons of the church at Carthage, one of whom was my highly esteemed friend and now colleague in the episcopate, Aurelius. He is the sole survivor of that group of guests, and I have often compared notes with him regarding this remarkable mercy of God and have found that his memory of the events corresponds with my own. Their visit, as usual, was in the evening, and Innocent begged them, with tearfulness in his voice, to please come the next day to what, he was sure, would be not merely his agony but his death [this is before the existence of effective anesthetics and patients were known to die of shock and pain during operations]. The very thought of the previous pains filled him with fear, and he was certain that he would die under the hands of the surgeons. Everyone tried to comfort him, and to exhort him to put his trust in God, and face His will unflinchingly.

Then we all began to pray. The rest of us prayed, as we usually do, on our knees and prostrate on the floor, but Innocent literally threw himself flat as though he had been violently struck by some powerful blow, and then burst into prayer so vehemently, so feelingly, so pathetically and wept with such indescribable groaning and sobbing that he shook in every fiber of his being and all but choked. How any of the others could pray, with all this pitiable petitioning to distract them, I do not know. As for myself, no formula of prayer was possible. All I could do was let my heart repeat this short refrain: "Lord, if Thou dost not hear such prayers, what prayers of any saints can move Thee?" It seemed to me that, with one more sigh, the poor man would have prayed himself to death. At last, we all arose and, when the bishop had given us his blessing, left. There was one final request that all would be present in the morning and, on our part, one last exhortation for the sufferer to have fortitude.

The dreaded day had hardly dawned when all these men of God were at the door to keep their promises. The doctors entered. The needed preparations were immediately under way. As each piece of frightening metal flashed, we gasped and held our breath. Then, while the patient's body was being properly disposed for the hand of the operating surgeon, Innocents's closest friends stood by, whispering words of comfort to cheer his drooping spirit. The bandages were removed. The site was exposed. The surgeon took a look. With the scalpel in one hand, he palpated for the offending sinus. He searched once more with his eye. He probed again with his fingers. He exhausted every means of medical examination. But there was nothing to be found except perfectly healthy tissue!

Imagine the burst of joy and the flood of grateful tears, and praise and thanks to the God of mercy and of power that broke from every one there present. It was a scene too much for any pen to tell. I can only leave it to the meditation of my readers.[3]

A little later in the same chapter, Augustine chronicles his realization of

how many miracles . . . [are] occurring in our own day and which [are] so like the miracles of old . . . It is only two years ago that the keeping of records was begun here

3. Ibid.

in Hippo, and already, at this writing, we have nearly seventy attested miracles. I know with certain knowledge of many others which have not, so far, been officially recorded.[4]

Writing later in *The Retractions*, Augustine again stressed the continuing occurrence of miracles and their importance in the life of the church.[5]

CASE 2

Pascal is well known not only as a major figure in the history of science who made influential contributions in both mathematics and physics, but also as the author of *Pensées* which, although it was never completed due to Pascal's early death, is a classic of Christian apologetics and contemplation. What is not so well known is that the dramatic healing of his niece, Marguerite Perrier was one of his primary motivations for writing the *Pensées*. Her healing is of further historical significance, inasmuch as it was the first of eighty reported healings that took place at the Jansenist monastery of Port-Royal. These healings were widely publicized and investigated. Although some were later shown to be fraudulent, others were supported by medical evidence and authenticated by diocesan authorities.[6] As was noted in the main body of this book, it was the Jansensist miracles that Hume refers to when he wrote,

> Many of the miracles were immediately proved upon the spot, before judges of unquestioned integrity, attested by witnesses of credit and distinction, in a learned age, and on the most eminent theatre that is now in the world. Nor is this all: a relation of them was published and dispersed everywhere; nor were the Jesuits, though a learned body, supported by the civil magistrate, and determined enemies to those opinions, in whose favour the miracles were said to have been wrought, ever able

4. Ibid., 445.

5. Augustine, *Retractions*; see, e.g., 1:12.7 and 1:13.5.

6. Brown, *Miracles and the Critical Mind*, 39.

distinctly to refute or detect them. Where shall we find such a number of circumstances, agreeing to the corroboration of one fact?[7]

Hume then went on to summarily dismiss the reports, writing,

What have we to oppose to such a cloud of witnesses, but the absolute impossibility or miraculous nature of the events, which they relate? And this surely, in the eyes of all reasonable people, will alone be regarded as a sufficient refutation.[8]

Marguerite Perrier, at the age of six, developed a condition known as a lachrymal fistula in the corner of her left eye next to her nose. This medical term means literally a channel from which tears and other bodily fluids continually leak. Pascal was present at the onset of her condition and describes it as beginning with "some drops of water which fell out of the corner of the said left eye next to the nose, the discharge rapidly growing more frequent and viscous and eventually changing into something like boue [mud]."[9]

Over the next few years, doctors who examined Mademoiselle Perrier recommended cauterization, but could give no assurance that her eye could be saved or that she would survive such a procedure. The family did not want to take such a serious risk and tried a number of less harsh remedies. None of these worked; the result being that the condition got worse to the degree that it was decided by the family in August 1655 to discontinue treatment in the hopes that her body would heal itself. This did not happen. Instead, a tumor formed and she lost her sense of smell and the fluid from the fistula began to flow into her nose and mouth to the extent that she had great difficulties eating, breathing and sleeping. She was at this time living in residence at a school associated with the Port-Royal monastery and the smell from this fluid was so bad that she had to be segregated from the other girls attending the school. By early March 1656, she had grown so weak and

7. Hume, *Enquiry Concerning Human Understanding*, 154.

8. Ibid.

9. Shiokawa, *Pascal et les miracles*, 79.

emaciated that the family was now willing to risk cauterization in the hopes that her life could be saved. The family began to make preparations for the operation.

On March 24, the Port-Royal monastery received on loan from Monsieur De la Potterie a relic purported to be a thorn from the crown of Christ. That evening, after vespers, the girls attending the school filed past the relic. When it came to be Mauguerite Perrier's turn, she was told by the schoolmistress, "Commend yourself to God and touch the thorn to your eye." She did so and returned to her room after the ceremony. She had scarcely reached her room when she said to one of the other girls, "My sister, I am no longer in pain. The holy thorn has cured me." What took place was described as follows:

> The source of the boue [mud] which was flowing continually from her eye, her nose and her mouth, and which had still been flowing on her cheek a moment before the miracle . . . was completely dried up. The bone, which had been decayed and rotten, was restored to its original condition. All the stench which had been associated with her wound, and which was so intolerable that the girl had to be separated from the others by order of the doctors and surgeons, was changed into breath as sweet as an infant's. At the same time she recovered her sense of smell, and none of the ills which were a result of the main one returned. Even her colour which had been pale and leaden, became as lively and clear at it ever had been.[10]

This healing became widely known to such an extent that the Queen Mother and the King of France sent their personal physicians to examine Mauguerite Perrier. These physicians, as well as other prominent doctors and religious authorities, investigated the healing in detail. Along with physicians who had treated her from the onset of her condition, they unanimously concluded there were no medical causes of her cure. Even the Jesuits, who were

10. Graeme Hunter notes that the author of this description of Mauguerite Perrier's healing may well have been the French philosopher Arnauld, who was closely associated with the Port-Royal monastery. "Arnauld's Defence of Miracles," 114–16.

determined theological enemies of the Jansenists, recognized that a miracle had occurred, confining their criticism to making the point that the miracle should not be taken as establishing the truth of the Jansenists's theological doctrines.[11]

CASE 3

A professor of engineering who, for reasons of privacy, wishes to withhold his name, agreed to contribute the following account. It is given in his own words:

I have personally seen God heal people essentially instantaneously in response to the prayers of a few "garden variety" Christians. These healings include "water on the ear" pain that was under active treatment through prescription medication, mononucleosis, and an accident-induced range of motion problem in a person's wrist. The venues where these healings occurred were a waterpark, a person's house, and a video store. The persons healed were a young girl, a middle-aged man, and a woman in her fifties. Here, I have chosen to report the story of my own healing because it is not as straightforward as those cases and because I have supporting medical records.

When I was in my first grade of school, one of my teachers recommended that I have a hearing test because I seemed to have trouble hearing. The visit to the audiologist proved to be the first of many that would, in a certain sense, characterize part of who I was as a child and young person. I was the kid who could not hear properly. I had a substantial unilateral hearing loss.

I was raised in an Evangelical, but not Charismatic church, and as a teenager I sought God repeatedly to heal my hearing; however, my hearing continued to slowly deteriorate.

My hearing deficit made it impossible for me to tell the direction from which sounds came, made it difficult for me to follow conversation in the presence of background sound, and prevented

11. Ibid.

me from experiencing music in "stereo." I had great difficulty recognizing people's voices on the telephone and I realized the degree to which I relied on lip reading when I would use video links or experience audio-visual media in which the video and sound tracks were not precisely synchronized.

When I was in my late forties, I suddenly became aware one morning that I could barely hear anything in my "good ear." At the time, I was holding an administrative position at the university where I teach engineering. An amplified phone was installed in my office, but it was of limited use because even when I turned up the volume to the point that it was painful to hold the handset to my ear, I still could not make out what the other person was saying. I would ask my secretary to write out my voice messages. In class, questions from students virtually stopped because I could not make out what they were asking, even when I was only a meter or two from them. My lip reading was not reliable enough to overcome the hearing problem. When I was lecturing, I could not tell how loud I was speaking.

My family doctor arranged appointments with a number of hearing specialists in my city and in Toronto. They did a suite of audio tests and, suspecting a brain tumor, carried out a CAT scan. These tests showed no physical cause for the hearing loss, but multiple approaches confirmed that the hearing loss was caused by auditory nerve degeneration. The tests showed that my hearing was below the threshold where a hearing aid would be of value and the doctors recommended that I consider having a cochlear implant.

I was desperate. Over the next six months, when I was in contact with any Christians who believed in healing, I had them pray for me. I had the elders of my church pray for me. I visited a number of churches within driving distance where healings were reported and had their ministry teams pray for me.

In time there seemed to be some improvement, but I wanted to know whether I was learning to cope with my situation or whether there was really an improvement. When I told my family doctor that I thought my hearing had improved she kindly but firmly reminded me that nerve damage does not heal. Perhaps to humor me, she arranged for another hearing test.

I remember the audiologist looking at the results of that test for several minutes before telling me in a somewhat puzzled voice that my hearing had indeed improved substantially. The tests showed that my hearing was nearly as good as it had been when I was much younger.

At the time of this writing, I still struggle at times with aspects of my remaining unilateral hearing deficiency. However, I now often recognize voices on the phone, I am frequently encouraged by new sounds that I hear in nature, and a few times recently I have been able to identify the direction from which a sound emanated.

To tell my story takes more that the five sentences needed to report many of the biblical miracles and the outcome of my story is less tidy. Instead, my story is one of process, unexplained setbacks, ongoing gratefulness and continuing hope.

October 13, 2007

It seems that my hearing has continued to improve gradually. I have been hearing an increasing range of sounds in nature, and I am better able to recognize and discriminate between the voices of different people.

July 16, 2014

CASE 4

I have written this account on the basis of an interview conducted with Mary Ellen Fitch on October 29, 2007.

At nineteen, Mary Ellen Fitch was living on the streets of Vancouver doing a great amount of drugs and alcohol. She awoke one morning from sleeping on the floor to find that friends had stolen her drugs. Initially, she was very angry, but then began to ask herself why she was living the way she was. Deciding she needed to make a fresh start, she went to the train station and was standing in line to leave the city. She had not yet settled on a destination when she saw a poster of an attractive hotel. When she asked the man selling tickets where the hotel was, he told her that it was located in Banff, Alberta. She arrived in Banff with a dollar and seventy-five cents, found a job as an elevator operator at the hotel she had seen on the poster and resolved to live drug and alcohol free.

She was largely successful in this, though she still continued to smoke marijuana. After three months she began to get sick. She got sicker and sicker and eventually was unable to make it to work. She went to a hospital where they diagnosed her with hepatitis B and immediately admitted her and put her in isolation. Her doctor informed her that she was seriously ill and would be in the hospital at least three months and most probably a year. He also told her that she would have permanent liver damage. Mary Ellen soon turned very yellow and her liver was swollen to such an extent that she appeared pregnant.

Although Mary Ellen believed in God, she was very angry with Him. Her brother had died when she was ten years old and her father died three years later. Her mother was very busy dealing with her own problems and trying to make a living, with the consequence that, from age thirteen on, Mary Ellen had been largely on her own, receiving little parental guidance or control. A little over a week into her treatment, Mary Ellen was unable to sleep at night because of pain. In the middle of the night she had an experience she describes as "coming face to face with God." She recalls feeling that she did not know whether it would be better to live or to die, but that she decided she would give her life to God and would let Him make that decision.

She was able to go to sleep after this experience, and, when she awoke the next morning and had blood tests, the tests revealed that her blood was normal. She was still weak and was kept in the hospital in isolation for the full incubation time. Upon her release, the doctor kept her coming back for further blood tests every week because he was puzzled how her blood could be registering as normal.

Mary Ellen identifies her healing as the beginning of her commitment to Christianity. She is now a middle-aged woman and has never had problems with her liver since.

CASE 5

This account is comprised of an email received from Margaret Thompson on Sept 20, 2009, regarding the healing of her son Aaron. I had spoken with Margaret several days before and, after hearing her account, asked her to write it up and send it to me in an email. She copied it to her son Aaron, so that if there were any corrections or omissions, he would contact me. He has indicated that he agrees with his mother's description of his healing.

Aaron, I spoke with Bob Larmer the other day [Sept. 17, 2009] at the credit union. He teaches philosophy at UNB [University of New Brunswick]. Somehow I got around to telling him about your miracle. I had no idea that Bob has been documenting miracles. He asked that I share our story. Love you, Mom.

Ellis, my husband, and I were blessed with two wonderful boys: Adrian was born on July 27, 1982, and Aaron was born on my birthday April 20, 1984. "My best birthday present ever!" is what I told him later. Both Adrian and Aaron went on to study engineering after high school . . . Adrian took civil engineering and then did his Masters right away too. He is working for GemTek in Moncton.

Aaron took mechanical engineering and graduated on the dean's list. After a few job interviews that were for supervisory roles alone, Aaron decided to return to UNB to get his teaching degree. One day I said to him (and I'm embarrassed now that I did!) "Aaron, why are you going into education? You can earn a lot more money as an engineer?" Aaron looked at me, and quickly responded, "Mom, as long as I'm doing what God wants me to do, what difference does it make how much money I earn?" So Aaron began classes at UNB in September 2007 and was to complete his BED degree in Dec 2008.

As I said earlier, Ellis and I are very blessed with boys who love the Lord, who are active in our church, and who have volunteered countless hours working with family and youth.

Around Feb 14, 2008, Aaron developed cold and flu like symptoms. He went to outpatients and the doctor told him to go home and rest and wait it out. Five days or so later, Aaron was not feeling better and went to outpatients again. His head was heavy and his eyes were sore. He felt miserable. The doctor gave him a heavy dose of medication for a deep rooted sinus infection and said that he definitely would not start feeling better for at least 5 days. But better days were ahead. Wait it out.

At this point in Aaron's illness, I went to New Orleans, USA, with 18 other people from our church to volunteer for a week. We were still trying to fix homes that had been damaged by Hurricane Katrina 2 1/2 years before that! We had a wonderful week, working hard, and getting to know fellow church members on a whole new level. Even there, I was surrounded by family: my (other) son, my brother, my brother-in-law, and my aunt were there with me as well! At the end of our week, we stood at the home of Mrs. Caroline and we sang with her "How Great Thou Art"! She was sure that God had finally sent his angels, after she had prayed for that for 2 1/2 years! We returned from our trip south in a snow storm, but with high spirits. We had been greatly blessed as we were being a blessing. What a feeling!

But things were not well at all with Aaron. His vision was getting worse, his coloring was gray . . . he reminded me of an AIDS patient. He was thin. I was very worried! Again we went to outpatients. This time, Dr. Brian MacKinnon saw him. Brian asked Aaron what lines he could see on the vision chart, and Aaron told him he couldn't see any of them. He could only see the outline of Brian's body. Brian immediately referred Aaron to an eye specialist, Dr. Harrison. Dr. Harrison looked into Aaron's eyes and shook his head. It wasn't good, we knew. He suggested that Aaron take steroid eye drops for a few days, and then come back to see him. We did that, but the results were no better. Dr. Harrison indicated retina damage, and wondered out loud about Lyme's disease. He said Aaron needed to go to Halifax ASAP. I was relieved! Finally, we would get the proper help!

Dr. Harrison called at 9:30 or so that evening (from home) and said the doctors in Halifax would be ready to see Aaron early the next afternoon. I figured I was going to Halifax, but no, Aaron had other plans. Adrian was doing his masters at UNB and was able to go to Halifax with his brother for 7 days. As a parent, it was *very* hard to be here, with our boys in Halifax, but we knew it was better. Our boys are close and were good company for each other. I went to work, with my bags packed, ready to drive to Halifax with a moment's notice, but that call never came. I begged God to give me the blindness, and to give Aaron my eyesight. He was too young and had so much potential. I sent emails to friends and family across Canada, USA, Holland, England, and Australia. Prayers were going up for Aaron all around the world! And if you don't believe in the power of prayer, well, read on!

Aaron was in hospital in Halifax for 7 days. Almost right away, he was diagnosed with bilateral uvieitis . . . infection in both eyes. Often when someone has bilateral uvieitis, they also have something else. So, Aaron was diagnosed for AIDS, Lymes disease, colitis, brain tumor, etc. After major doses of steroids and antibiotics and lots of testing, the news from the doctors was grim: Because Aaron had not seen an eye specialist sooner, and because retina damage is permanent (it cannot be "fixed" with glasses or with surgery), Aaron was told he would never drive again, he would never be an engineer, he would likely never be a teacher . . . They suggested he contact CNIB [Canadian National Institute for the Blind] and get on with his life. Even after receiving this news, Aaron held fast to his faith and knew that God was in control. But the reality of never seeing again was becoming more real. What was he to do with his education studies at the University of New Brunswick? Could he catch up on his studies to become a teacher? At that point, he definitely did not feel well enough to do so.

Cheryl, Aaron's girlfriend, drove to Halifax, from PEI where she taught at a Christian school, to visit Aaron in the hospital. She visited him again a weekend later at home. I was at work late

Monday afternoon, when Aaron called me with a "question." He wondered what I thought of the idea of Cheryl and him getting married! I said "WHAT????????? Does she know what she is getting herself into? She'll have to drive you around for the next 60 years!" This is a miracle in itself, I would say, that a young lady will make a lifelong commitment to marry someone just diagnosed with legal blindness! A few hours later, my husband and I sat at Swiss Chalet enjoying supper with the newly engaged couple!

God did not grant Aaron an instant miracle of the restoration of his sight, it was gradual. Two months after the doctors in Halifax said he would *never* see again and he would *never* drive again and he would *never* be a mechanical engineer, Aaron accepted a job as a mechanical engineer for KanGoRoo Playgrounds in Atholville near Campbellton, NB!

On May 31, 2008, we moved both of our boys as they went to work as engineers . . . Aaron to Atholville and Adrian to Moncton. And very quickly we felt the pain of the empty nest! We were very proud of both of them, but would have loved for them to live and work closer to home. However, God knows best.

On Thanksgiving Sunday, 2008, Aaron spoke in church, thanking God for his blindness and for the miracle of having his sight restored again. What a testimony! He thanked all present for their encouragement, prayers and support.

On December 30, 2009, Aaron and Cheryl were married. Again, after all the ups and downs of the past year, and the witness to God's unfailing faithfulness, we celebrated this very special day surrounded by family and friends.

Unbeknownst to us, Aaron told Cheryl on the way home from their honeymoon that he felt called to go into the ministry. We found out about this in February 2009. Instantly, I sank into a depression. It was hard enough with our boys 2 hours and 4 hours away, but now he was going to be 25 hours away! And if they were ever to make us grandparents, how far away would they be from us?

I came up with lots of excuses why Aaron shouldn't go . . . foremost financially. In the meantime, Aaron applied to Calvin

Seminary and waited for an answer. Three or four days before he got an answer from the college, someone from the admissions office called him at home and suggested he fill out an application for the presidential scholarship. He was a prime candidate because of his volunteer work with our church youth group and boys group, and with his involvement in the worship praise team. Aaron talked to us about "staying up late a few nights" to apply for this scholarship, but the hours paid off big time! He was awarded the Presidential scholarship of $10,000 per year as long as he maintained a 3.5 grade point average. He should be able to do that . . . after all, he was on the dean's list for mechanical engineering!

It is estimated that the cost of a married couple to be at Calvin College is about 30K per year. Our church denomination will sponsor him about 12K, his scholarship is 10K, and if required, Aaron's father in law said he would pay the balance! So much for my argument of financial hardship being a deterrent!

Aaron and Cheryl moved to Grand Rapids, Michigan, USA, on August 20, 2009. Aaron has been in class now for 4 weeks and thoroughly loves it! Cheryl's family live only 3 hours away in Sarnia, Ontario. God is good. Very good. He has granted us two miracles . . . the restoration of Aaron's eyesight (he was tested in Dec 2008 and his vision is 20/20) and Aaron has a wonderful wife and life partner in Cheryl.

We have been very blessed. To God be the glory!
Margaret and Ellis Thompson

CASE 6

I asked Dr. Joseph Novak to contribute the following account. It is given in his own words with no editing on my part. Dr. Novak, now retired, formerly taught philosophy at the University of Waterloo. His research interests are in the areas of Ancient and Medieval Philosophy.

For many years my mother, Mary Novak, had suffered with leg ulcers. She began to be afflicted by these after she had injured her left leg. Although she was not diabetic—diabetes is often but not always a causal factor in circulatory problems of the legs—the ulcers were persistent and required medical attention. Over the years various types of medicated pads and salves were administered, along with the strict injunction that my mother stay off her feet as much as possible. Although my mother scrupulously followed the treatment regime which included almost daily whirlpooling of the legs and changing of bandages, she was not as cooperative in the area of rest. Being a very active person, she would practically never sit back, prop up her legs, and give them the rest they needed.

Her problem stretched over many years, having begun sometime in the early 1990s. On various occasions she was hospitalized or did a stay in a nursing home if the ulcers became badly inflected. In retrospect it seems that the whirlpooling was probably contributing to this, as one doctor intimated later. During these periods she would have her legs treated with antibiotics that were administered orally or intravenously.

This state of affairs seemed to one from which she seem unable to escape. At those times when the ulcers seemed well on their way to disappearing, a new infection would set in, the ulcers would grow larger, and all progress appeared lost.

A crisis arose in the Spring of 1999, however. My mother had suffered a fall in her condo apartment in Oak Lawn, Illinois, where she had been living at the time. After being x-rayed, she was told that by the technician that there was a fracture in her femur but, in his opinion, it did not warrant surgery. The physician in charge, however, thought it did require surgery. With some reluctance, my mother agreed to the surgery which, as far as the femur was concerned, proved to be successful.

However, there was a devastating side effect. Since her right leg, the leg then afflicted with some ulceration, was put in traction for the surgery, there appeared to have been a restriction of blood flow to the already suffering leg. Later, one of her doctors stated that even if the traction had not caused the problem, the operation on the upper part of the leg, by itself, would have easily restricted blood flow to the lower part of the leg due to the ensuing swelling. Within a very short time gangrene set in on a large scale—the instep, heel, and extensive areas near them were covered with gangrene. The doctors attending her recommended amputation of the leg below the knee, although they were not entirely confident (as they confided to my sister and me) that she would survive the operation given her weakened condition and her age (she was then 81). My mother was informed of their evaluation and she refused the surgery. She stated that she had come into the world with two legs and that she would leave the world with both of them.

The doctors informed my sister and me that there was nothing further that they could do, that her condition was terminal, and that we should make arrangements with hospice. They dismissed her from the hospital in Harvey, Illinois, into a nursing home of our choosing which was in Westmont, Illinois. Her condition was very serious. She had lost considerable weight—down from a maximum of approximately 120 lbs. to about 86 lbs. She refused medication (apart from the pain medication and, I believe, blood thinners which the staff administered). Much of her leg, extending from about six inches below the knee was covered with bandages. There was a small area left exposed on the bottom of her foot near the toes. The visible part of the leg had become grey and its texture seemed to be degenerating (i.e., it appeared "netted" and losing firmness). Just beneath the back of the toes there were three distinct small round black spots. I presumed this was where part of the traction device had made contact.

Upon arrival at the nursing home my mother was assigned a new doctor, the one who attended all the patients. Her previous doctors had ended their supervision of her, having abandoned her to hospice with a terminal diagnosis. The only attention her leg was given involved a regular changing of the bandages. The foul odor the leg was emitting was noticeable to the nursing staff.

At this point I called a woman in St. Louis, Missouri, with whom I was acquainted, and who was involved in a Christian healing ministry. Her name is Joan Gieson. She is known in the St.

Louis area for her work with the poor, the homeless, and the sick. She is also known for the annual Christmas dinner she puts on for the poor, a dinner that usually feeds upwards of 17,000 people. I telephoned her long distance and described to her the extent of my mother's problem. My intention in calling her was simply to request that she keep the whole situation in prayer. However, I was totally surprised by her response. She asked whether I wanted her to fly to Chicago to pray for my mother. I told her that I myself would be delighted but that I had, of course, to ask my mother. I expected my mother would reply in like manner, since my mother was a person of faith, had seen Joan minister both at services of healing and on television. I called again to St. Louis and conveyed to Joan the positive response that my mother gave me. Although Joan offered to pay for her flight with her accumulated air miles, I insisted that I would cover the expense. We then and there made a booking with Southwest Airlines via means of a conference call.

I picked Joan up at Midway Airport in Chicago on Friday morning, May 21, 1999. I had asked my cousin Ron Mazany and his mother, my Aunt Stephanie, to be present at the nursing home that day to be supportive both physically, emotionally, and spiritually. I wanted someone to be there in the morning to help my mother get prepared for the visit since I would be required to go to the airport to get Joan Gieson. My sister who had come to the nursing home up to that point on a daily basis had told me she would not be present that morning. She was unaware of what I had arranged and her upcoming absence was a relief to me. My sister was not especially open to the possibility of spiritual healing and certainly did not believe that anything miraculous could transpire at this late stage of events. I was aware that the atmosphere around a person who needs healing is a matter of concern. Mark 6 tells of the inability of Jesus (*ouk edunato*) to perform miracles in a location due to the local unbelief; Mark 5 tells of Jesus "throwing out" (*ekbalon*) those who laughed at the prospect of raising Jairus' daughter and surrounding himself only with the parents and close disciples.

I took Joan to a conference room at the nursing home because it seemed we would not have the privacy required in my
mother's room which was shared with another patient. In the process of getting my mother into a wheel chair to bring her to the
conference room, my mother stubbed one of her toes. This caused
prolonged bleeding due to the blood thinners she was or had been
receiving; it also caused a delay in bringing her to the conference
room. Finally my mother was wheeled in, the five of us were alone
and Joan read to my mother a portion of Ephesians 1, emphasizing
verse 5: "by which He made us accepted in the Beloved." Only later
did I fully appreciate how needed that message was for my mother.
We then sang a hymn, Joan laid hands on my mother. My mother
returned to her room, my aunt and cousin returned to their home,
and I took Joan back to Midway. Due to the delays at the nursing
home, Joan missed her originally scheduled Southwest Airlines
flight. However, it was a welcomed delay for me, since we had an
opportunity to chat.

The following day my sister returned for a visit to the nursing home. She was not told of Joan's visit. My mother had insisted
that she herself would decide when to tell my sister and it was not
until considerably later that my sister learned of what had trans-
pired. However, among the first things my sister said after she ap-
proached my mother's bed was that the leg looked better. Indeed,
it did. The exposed part of the leg seemed to have changed from its
dingy grey color and the texture of the skin had improved. I visited
my mother every day during this period; I stayed in her condo in
Oak Lawn and made the 25 minute drive up the Interstate 294 to
Westmont (on Ogden). On Tuesday following Joan's visit I noticed
the three black spots on the exposed part of the sole on the affected
leg had changed color from black to red. Subsequently these spots
would disappear entirely. My mother's health was improving. The
nurses noted that the smell from the leg was not as bad as it had
been. Gradually the gangrene started to drop off.

The nursing home doctor and his assistant were astonished
at the transformation as was an additional doctor who had con-
sulted with them after my mother's admission to the nursing home

facility. My mother spent several months at the facility—the gangrene had been extensive, it took a long time for tissue to begin to replace the affected area, and it took some therapy to get her up and about and moving again. The facility did not want to release her until they were certain she could be returned home safely. My mother returned home in time for Thanksgiving in November of that year.

There is much more that could be told. In brief, my mother lived till April 2, 2005, when she succumbed to the effects of a stroke she had had in late February, a few weeks earlier. There was still a bit of the wound that needed to be closed before the stroke occurred, but no gangrene ever returned, despite the fact that my mother badly bumped one of her toes on that foot in her condo during this six year period.

My own interest in divine healing goes back to my youth. I had the privilege of attending the services of many great healing ministers, such as Kathryn Kuhlman and Kenneth Hagin, among others. Joan Gieson had herself worked for the Kuhlman ministry. I became acquainted with Maudie Phillips of Brockville, Ontario, who was the Kuhlman representative in Canada up to the time of Kuhlman's death. After my transfer to Ontario in the mid 1980s I was able to visit Maudie and her husband Harvey at their home on several occasions. Had it not been for this familiarity with the Kuhlman ministry, I would probably never have made the acquaintance of Joan Gieson and my mother would probably never have received the healing that she did.

Throughout these decades I sat through many a healing meeting and learned a great deal. Of course, some ministries were more smoke than fire. Some ministers were frauds, some were more emotional than genuinely spiritual, some were sincere but confused, but some were sincere and effectual. Practically none were—if I be allowed to pronounce the indubitable, unquestionable, and always accurate judgment of a philosopher!—perfect. However, I came to realize that God uses imperfect instruments to do His work—as even the current head of the Roman Church stated during his inaugural speech in reference to his own election

("The fact that the Lord knows how to work and to act even with inadequate instruments [*con instrumenti insufficienti*] comforts me," April 19, 2005). This means, of course, that God's work is often only imperfectly realized. Kenneth Hagin often said that success in healing depended on two factors: the degree of healing power administered and the acceptance of the person receiving the healing. Nevertheless, despite human imperfection, marvelous things occur. I have witnessed and experienced many astonishing "wonders" (as the Scriptures designate miracles).

It is the nature of an academic to be critical and skeptical. The Greek etymology of the term "skeptical" is that of "looking at, or examining, something with care." Many academics claim that they are reluctant to accept any reports of the miraculous without documentary evidence. Such documentary evidence does exist— consider the work of Dr. Casdorph whose study *The Miracles*[12] contain many records in support of healing claims. There are, as well, other documentary studies that exist. However, if one begins to visit or inhabit the communities or situations where miracles are occurring, written evidence pales in comparison to actual events. The experiences I have had with many believing Christians over the years has put the reality of these types of events beyond doubt for me.

Although I have probably gone on too long, I would like to venture a few remarks from a philosophical point of view. Of course, as a philosopher, I have had many questions about miraculous events, how they occur, what is the Biblical teaching about miracles, what role faith plays, how does God work in these manifestations, and so forth. What appear to be anomalies in Nature may very well be simply the regularities of the Kingdom. In speaking with a Christian sociologist who was attending a meeting at which I was present (I believe the meeting took place at Calvin College many years ago), we discussed the famous "Toronto Airport" phenomenon. (For those unfamiliar with this, the Toronto Airport Fellowship is a charismatic community once referred to as the "Toronto Vineyard" due to its former association with the John

12. Casdorph, *Miracles*, 1976.

Wimber association of churches). She noted that the conference speakers were all involved with the "head thing," i.e., they were highly critical of phenomena they had never witnessed, phenomena that just would not fit into their theoretical constructions. For many Christian philosophers and theologians the concept of faith has been so deeply shaped by modern epistemological debates that the productive type of faith that miracles depend on for their occurrence seems to elude them. For the philosopher miracles are often seen as "proofs" or "warrants" for certain creedal articles. The purpose of miracles comes to be understood as establishing doctrine. Once doctrines are established, miracles are no longer needed. Hence the emergence of cessationist teaching concerning miracles and the justification for their scarcity.

This whole picture is untenable for anyone who reads the Scriptures carefully. Everything about the Christian life is miraculous. Each prayer, each act of faith, every conversion is a miracle. This holds for every believer, all over the world (and perhaps elsewhere). What Hume says with cynicism, the believer holds with sincerity: faith is a miracle. When faith is seen as an active power ("mountain-moving faith") and not merely as an intellectual assent to a proposition warranted on the basis of its divine origin, the operation of miracles becomes realizable. What is akin, in the natural domain, to bringing about miracles is not the faith, i.e., "assent," of a speculative thinker but the faith, i.e., "commitment" of a practicing investigator. Just as the "real assurance" of Thomas Edison sustained him through thousands of failed trials to find the appropriate filament to make the light bulb glow, so the sustained assurance that God deeply desires healing in a particular case will bring about a miracle.

However, I have gone on too long. Prof. Larmer has examined the real and thorny questions involved with this issue from a quite legitimate and important philosophical standpoint. My hope is that this testimony of a particular healing will assure the reader that the topic he has undertaken to write about with such care is not a mere fancy but one deserving your attention.

FOR FURTHER READING

Brown, Colin. *Miracles and the Critical Mind*. Grand Rapids: Eerdmans, 1984.

Burns, R. M. *The Great Debate on Miracles*. East Brunswick, NJ: Associated University Presses, 1981.

Campbell, George. *Dissertation on Miracles*. Edinburgh: 1762. 3rd ed., 2 vols., Edinburgh, 1797.

Casdorph, H. Richard. *The Miracles*. Plainfield, NJ: Logos International, 1976.

Collins, C. John. *The God of Miracles*. Wheaton, IL: Crossway, 2000.

Corner, Mark. *Signs of God*. Burlington, VT: Ashgate, 2005.

Earman, John. *Hume's Abject Failure*. Oxford: Oxford University Press, 2000.

Flew, Antony. *Hume's Philosophy of Belief*. London: Routledge & Paul, 1961.

Fogelin, Robert J. *A Defense of Hume on Miracles*. Princeton, NJ: Princeton University Press, 2003.

Geivett, R. Douglas, and Gary R. Habermas, eds. *In Defence of Miracles*. Downers Grove: InterVarsity, 1997.

Grant, R. M. *Miracle and Natural Law in Graeco-Roman and Early Christian Thought*. Amsterdam: North Holland, 1952.

Houston, Joseph. *Reported Miracles*. Cambridge: Cambridge University Press, 1994.

Hume, David. "Of Miracles." In *An Enquiry Concerning Human Understanding*. Edited by Antony Flew. La Salle, IL: Open Court, 1988.

Jaki, Stanley L. *Miracles and Physics*. Front Royal, VA: Christendom, 2004.

Keener, Craig. *Miracles: The Credibility of the New Testament Accounts*. Grand Rapids: Baker, 2011.

Larmer, Robert. *The Legitimacy of Miracle*. New York: Lexington, 2014.

Lewis, C. S. *Miracles*. London: Fontana, 1974.

MacNutt, Francis. *Healing*. Notre Dame: Ave Maria, 1974. Rev. ed., 1999.

Moule, C. F. D., ed. *Miracles: Cambridge Studies in Their Philosophy and History*. London: Mowbray, 1965.

Mozley, J. B. *Eight Lectures on Miracles*. London: Longmans, Green, 1890.

Mullin, Robert Bruce. *Miracles and the Modern Religious Imagination*. London: Yale University Press, 1996.

For Further Reading

Newman, John Henry. *Two Essays on Biblical and on Ecclesiastical Miracles.* London: Longmans, Green, 1890.

Sherlock, Thomas. *The Trial of the Witnesses of the Resurrection of Jesus.* 1st ed., 1729. 8th ed., London, 1736.

Swinburne, Richard. *The Concept of Miracle.* New York: Macmillan, 1970.

Tweyman, Stanley, ed. *Hume on Miracles.* Chicago: St. Augustine's, 1996.

Whately, Richard. *Historic Doubts Concerning the Existence of Napoleon Bonaparte.* 2nd ed. London: Routledge, 1890.

Wimber, John, and Kevin Springer. *Power Healing.* New York: HarperOne, 2009.

Bibliography

Augustine. *City of God*. Fathers of the Church 24. Washington, DC: Catholic University of America Press, 1954.

———. *Of True Religion*. In *Earlier Writings*, translated by John H. S. Burleigh. Library of Christian Classics 6. Philadelphia: Westminster, 1953.

———. *The Retractions*. Washington, DC: Catholic University of America Press, 1968.

Borg, Marcus J. *Jesus, a New Vision: Spirit, Culture, and the Life of Discipleship*. New York: Harper Collins, 1987.

Brown, Colin. *Miracles and the Critical Mind*. Grand Rapids: Eerdmans, 1984.

Burns, R. M. *The Great Debate on Miracles*. London: Associated University Presses, 1981.

Casdorph, H. Richard. *The Miracles*. Bellingham, WA: Logos International, 1976.

Gardner, Rex. *Healing Miracles: A Doctor Investigates*. London: Darton, Longman & Todd, 1986.

Hume, David. "Of Miracles." In *An Enquiry Concerning Human Understanding*, edited by Antony Flew, 143–66. La Salle, IL: Open Court, 1988.

Hunter, Graeme. "Arnauld's Defence of Miracles." In *Interpreting Arnauld*, edited by Elmar J. Kremer, 111–26. Toronto: University of Toronto Press, 1996.

Jaki, Stanley L. *Miracles and Physics*. Front Royal, VA: Christendom, 1986.

Keener, Craig S. *Miracles: The Credibility of the New Testament Accounts*. 2 vols. Grand Rapids: Baker Academic, 2011.

Larmer, Robert. *The Legitimacy of Miracle*. New York: Lexington, 2014.

Shiokawa, Tetsuya. *Pascal et les miracles*. Paris: Nizet, 1977.

Troeltsch, Ernst. "On the Historical and Dogmatic Methods in Theology." In *Religion in History*, translated by James Luther Adams and Walter E. Bense, 11–32. Minneapolis: Fortress, 1991.

CPSIA information can be obtained
at www.ICGtesting.com
Printed in the USA
LVHW022008291120
672955LV00012B/1656